SUBSCRIPTIONS

All issues from SCINTILLA 16 onward can be purchased through Amazon.com or Amazon.co.uk. For convenience, we hope to make back issues available through Amazon in future. Issues 1–15 are available directly from The Vaughan Association. Please email subscriptions@vaughanassociation.org to get further details.

*

WEBSITE

www.vaughanassociation.org

EMAIL

subscriptions@vaughanassociation.org

Submissions for Scintilla 25

Please submit critical articles on literature in the metaphysical tradition to prose@vaughanassociation.org.

Please submit new poetry for consideration through the poetry submission portal on our website:
http://www.vaughanassociation.org/submissions-to-scintilla/

All submissions are peer reviewed

SCINTILLA
The Journal of the Vaughan Association
24

This speech made me quickly look up to those glittering *Turrets of Salt*, where I could see a stupendous *Cataract*, or *Waterfall*. The *streame* was more *large* than any *River* in her full *Channell*, but not withstanding the *Height*, and *Violence* of its *Fall*, it descended without any *Noyse*. The *Waters* were *dash'd*, and their *Currents* distracted by those *Saltish Rocks*, but for all this they came down with a dead *silence*, like the still soft *Ayr*.
                    Thomas Vaughan, *Lumen de Lumine*

With what deep murmurs through times silent stealth
Doth thy transparent, cool and watry wealth
       Here flowing fall,
       And chide, and call,
As if his liquid, loose Retinue staid
Lingring, and were of this steep place afraid,
                    Henry Vaughan, 'The Water-fall'

A journal of literary criticism, prose and new poetry
in the metaphysical tradition

Published by
The Vaughan Association

© Copyright remains with the author

Published in 2021
Scintilla is a publication of The Vaughan Association

Essays in each issue of *Scintilla* frequently originate in talks first given at The Vaughan Association's annual Colloquium held each spring near the Vaughans' birth-place at Newton Farm near Llansantffraed, Breconshire.

All rights reserved. No part of this publication may be reproduced, stored in a retrieval system, or transmitted, in any form or by any means, electronic, mechanical, photocopying, recording or otherwise, without the prior permission of The Vaughan Association.

ISBN: 9798700554169
ISSN: 1368-5023

Published with the financial support of the Welsh Books Council

General Editor: Joseph Sterrett
Poetry Editors: Damian Walford Davies and Katherine Stansfield
Prose Editor: Erik Ankerberg
Reviews Editor: Elizabeth Ford
Editorial Assistant: Helena Short

Editorial Board:
Alan Rudrum
Donald Dickson
Helen Wilcox
Robert Wilcher

Advisors:
John Barnie, Robert Minhinnick, M. Wynn Thomas

Art Work:
David Brown

Typeset in Wales by JS Typesetting Ltd, Porthcawl
Printed by Kindle Direct Publishing

Contents

Preface	 vii	
Philip West	James Shirley and Henry Vaughan.........	1
Patrick Deeley	The Absence	24
Claire Scott	That Day in Hades...................	25
	Wings...........................	26
Christopher Norris	As Knowing Goes	27
Amanda Attfield	Exodus..........................	29
	Looking West at Birches Farm.......	30
Susan Wallace	Earth Work	32
	Beached........................	33
Graham High	Tilting at Windmills...............	34
	Green Man	35
Greg Miller	Scythe	36
Robert Wilcher	Henry Vaughan's Use of Biblical Epigraphs in *Silex Scintillans*........	37
Paul Connolly	Mass	56
	Spring Morning..................	58
Charles Wilkinson	archaeologists in the air............	59
	Submarine off Wales	60
	hantant	61
Ric Hool	Sky Burial	62
Margaret Wilmot	New Year.......................	63
	Fritillaries......................	64
Roger Garfitt	The Good Son	65
Sam Garvan	Three Rivers	66
Howard Wright	The Good Suit...................	69
	Everything......................	70
William Tate	Labor of Love: Richard Wilbur's 'A Plain Song for Comadre'.........	71

Michael Henry	The Authority Of Death	82
Helen Overell	Mending	83
	Three Yellow Butterflies	84
Jock Stein	Exodus	85
Eve Jackson	When the World Was Quiet	86
	Beyond a Dream	87
Matthew Stewart	In the Middle	88
Jonathan Wooding	The Book of Jashar	89
Tom Gouthwaite	Quiet Space	91
Lesley Saunders	Croquembouche	92
	Placebo	93
Jonathan Nauman	Holiness From Abroad: George Herbert's Dialogue with St. François and Henry Vaughan's Emulation of St. Paulinus	94
Thor Bacon	Little Fugue on the Hands	112
	Mowing After a Week of Rain	113
Martin Bennett	Above the Forum	114
	Tropical Stopover	115
Jeremy Hooker	A philosopher in search of the soul	116
Isabel Bermudez	Spring wood	118
	Honesty	120
Rachel Carney	Legerdemain	121
Sarah Lindon	Present tense	122
	I forget but nothing else does	123
Peter Limbrick	Lizard	124
Rosie Jackson	Thinking of Simone Weil	125
Greg Miller	Review: *David Jones: Engraver, Soldier, Painter, Poet*	127
Contributors		133

Preface

What are the ways that a poet relates to the words of other writers? Echoes perhaps from texts, points of conversation, or phrases captured through attention to rivals, friends, acquaintances and heroes. It's the language category literary critics broadly lump together as 'discourse'. *Scintilla 24* serendipitously pursues these subtle indications of word exchange in the work of Henry Vaughan, both in his contemporaries and in the ongoing effect that his language has had on poets that have followed. An abiding concern of the journal has been to trace the connectedness of the twin Vaughan brothers, Henry and Thomas, to the land they called their home, the undulating hills, wildlife, and breathtaking beauty, history and myth of the Usk Valley in Breaconshire. Their shared experiences, the devastation of loss in the civil wars, the destruction of so many familiar social, political and religious structures, left their mark as the men struggled to maintain an identity and continuity of faith. The men's reinvention of themselves in these shifting circumstances, Henry as the 'Silurist' and Thomas as 'Eugenius Philalethes', pressed their creative energy, forcing them to explore their sense of identity, adversity, and creativity itself in their writing. *Scintilla 24* probes such subtle conjunctions, crossing boundaries between past and present, between place and vision, our physical environment and our inner lives, between metaphysical experiences and the language of science, poetry, and healing.

Philip West listens attentively to the echoes in Henry's poetry that correspond with his contemporary and fellow Royalist, the playwright James Shirley. West traces surprising similarities which approach, if they do not quite achieve, a sense of literary intercourse between the two writers. Vaughan has frequently been noted to have a magpie tendency in his poetic borrowings, so West's examination of the concentric London literary circles both writers moved within are suggestive not only of Vaughan's early influences and perspective but of the wider cultural environment that would inform his later work. In a similar vein, Robert Wilcher gives focus to Vaughan's borrowings by examining his biblical allusiveness, particularly those used in his epigraphs. Vaughan, Wilcher notes, moves from employing the Bible as an authoritative source, to a more assured sense of an audience who share his familiarity with its words, a world imbued with a knowledge of scripture. Jonathan Nauman examines further Vaughan's interest in the devotional writing of St. Paulinus of Nola, developed out of Vaughan's admiration of George Herbert. Nauman outlines an intriguing number of careful (and carefully concealed) literary interests of George Herbert that, coming at a later day, his disciple Henry Vaughan explores more deeply. François de Sales, the 16th century Roman Catholic Bishop of Geneva who, though a Catholic evangelist, engaged in ironical discussions with such arch partisans as Theodore Beza. His writing provided surprising devotional inspiration for Herbert that led the way for Vaughan's attention to St. Paulinus. William Tate explores the work of another metaphysical poet, from 20th century America, Richard Wilbur, a first for *Scintilla*. Finding links to George Herbert and Gerard Manley Hopkins among other poets and writers, Tate examines Wilbur's sanctification of work, what Herbert describes as 'drudgerie divine', service both to man and God.

Contemporary poetry continues to feature in *Scintilla* and we are delighted to offer a wealth of new work exploring themes and motifs which resonate with the activities and preoccupations of the Vaughans. These poems were submitted, and selected, during the pandemic, and it's perhaps no surprise that in this work, read at this time, loss seems sharply present. Michael Henry's moving poem 'The Authority of Death' reflects on an elderly man with 'prophet-white hair and beard' teaching the speaker of the poem to drive. This is a potent memory when the older man's health fails, his strength 'stalling', but he remains 'livid not to live'.

Such tenacity for persevering is at the heart of Helen Overell's poem 'Mending' which reminds us that 'Amidst the chaos' there can be found 'new growth that shields old hurt, the in-built healing'. For many of the poets featured in this issue, it is the natural world which provides a healing touchstone. Sam Garvan, in the marvellously poised 'Three Rivers', captures the totemic power of flora and fauna seen in many of the poems in this issue: 'in the milkwort, all-seeing, / an egret waits for everything to pass'. Such an image seems all the more resonant after a year in which life has quietened to such a degree that more people have become aware of birdsong, and wildlife has greater visibility in our empty public spaces. Poetry, too, can occupy spaces in our lives that feel empty, helping us frame and articulate absences of all kinds.

James Shirley and Henry Vaughan

PHILIP WEST

When Henry Vaughan came to London in the early 1640s to study law – the precise dates seem locked in uncertainty, but at some point during 1640–2 – James Shirley was the most prominent dramatist in London, having succeeded his friend, the late Philip Massinger, as chief writer for the King's Men in April 1640. Shirley's appointment came at the end of four frustrating years attempting to establish a professional theatre company in Dublin, a post he had taken after plague closed London theatres in 1636, at the invitation of his university friend John Ogilby, now Master of the Revels to the Lord Deputy of Ireland, Sir Thomas Wentworth (later Earl of Strafford). While writing both for the Werburgh Street theatre and for entertainments at Dublin Castle, Shirley took what opportunities he had to return to London, overseeing publication of his plays, visiting his family, and unsuccessfully promoting himself for the role of Poet Laureate, which had fallen vacant in 1637 with the death of Ben Jonson. Shirley's young family lived in Rose Lane in Holborn, a location close to the law schools of the Inns of Court, in whose literary circles Shirley had mixed since the late 1620s, and where Vaughan also lived and studied after his arrival in London – having been, as he wrote to Aubrey, 'designed by my father for the study of the Law'.[1]

Could Vaughan have seen a performance of one of Shirley's plays during his time in London – perhaps *The Cardinal*, the tragedy first performed at Blackfriars in November 1641 (and successfully revived at the Southwark Playhouse in 2017)? Speculation aside, there was unquestionably plenty of Shirley's work in the repertory at this time: by September 1642, when the theatres were shut by

---

1 *The Works of Henry Vaughan*, ed. by Donald R. Dickson, Alan Rudrum, and Robert Wilcher, 3 vols (Oxford: Oxford University Press, 2018), vol. III, p. 800. All references to Vaughan's poems will be to this edition.

Parliament until 1660, Shirley had composed almost 50 plays and entertainments, most of which were performed not by the King's Men's but by their rivals, the companies formed by Christopher Beeston that performed at the Phoenix or Cockpit. Shirley's move to the King's Men in 1640 was prestigious, and must have been very welcome after the disappointments of Dublin. While we can only speculate whether Vaughan ever attended a play by Shirley, it seems likely that, like many law students, he took an active interest in the theatre; and, as Alan Rudrum has noted, Vaughan's early poems 'show that [he] had read or heard the Jacobean dramatists with attention', and it is certainly not an unreasonable assumption that he may have attended a performance of one of Shirley's plays – though of course another matter to suggest that he enjoyed or remembered it![2] More certain is that neither writer knew, as *The Cardinal* held the stage in November 1641, that within a year their literary careers would have been forever changed by the outbreak of war, nor that they would by that point be joining royalist armies – Shirley joining his patron, the Earl of Newcastle, at his headquarters in Newark, Vaughan fighting under Sir Herbert Price in Wales.

To draw Vaughan and Shirley together in this way is in no sense to suggest an ongoing or significant connection between the two, but rather to see what light each can cast light on the other, within the rapidly changing world of the early 1640s. Two main points of intersection between their writing careers are revealing and will provide the focus of this essay: firstly, the early 1640s, when both men were living west of London, and when, as I will suggest, Vaughan may have read a number of Shirley's poems with profit; and secondly, the year 1646, when both would print their poetry for the first time – Vaughan in his *Poems, with the tenth Satyre of Iuvenal Englished* (London: for G. Badger), and Shirley in his *Poems &c.* (London: for Humphrey Moseley). As I will suggest, a reader comparing the two books in 1646 might have sensed echoes of the established poet in the work of the young newcomer, alongside Vaughan's ingenious borrowings from, and imitations of, writers such as Thomas Randolph and William Habington. This article suggests a few moments of resemblance, but also seeks to revise the critical opposition that might be felt to exist between the more radical Vaughan – whose embracing of the task of writing 'true hymns' to God would shortly see him reject the social modes of Caroline lyric

---

2 Alan Rudrum, 'Vaughan, Henry (1621–1695)', in *The Oxford Dictionary of National Biography* (Oxford: Oxford University Press, 2004).

– and the ageing dramatist and lyricist who, if he is written about at all in modern criticism, is generally associated with old-fashioned ideas of 'cavalier' style. In fact, Shirley's *Poems &c.* was itself a revisionary work, critical of Caroline poetics, which it sought to dismantle in a spirit of attempted renewal that was closer in spirit to the sophisticated generic reworkings of Milton's *Poems* (1645) or the critical intelligence of Marvell's pastoral poetry. Charles was losing the first Civil War even as Shirley prepared *Poems &c.* for the press, but the book was not simply an exercise in royalist nostalgia. Rather, it was an attempted act of poetic renovation whose roots lay as far back as the late 1630s, and which in 1646 found a champion in the figure of Shirley's youthful patron, the poet and philosopher Thomas Stanley – whose own reading of Shirley's *Poems &c.* is our best cue to understanding Shirley's aims and intentions in publishing them.

*

At whatever time Vaughan arrived in London, James Shirley would have been the capital's leading dramatist: the writer of dozens of successful comedies and tragicomedies of London life since 1625, and newly enthroned as chief writer for the most prestigious London acting company. In the legal and literary world into which Vaughan had entered, Shirley was also widely reputed as the author of *The Triumph of Peace*, an elaborate and extravagant masque whose two successful performances before Charles and Henrietta Maria in 1634 had been a huge coup for the Inns of Court, as well as bringing Shirley the personal reward of being made an honorary member of Gray's Inn. *Triumph* had constituted, in part, the legal world's restitution to the crown for the offence caused by the lawyer William Prynne, whose denunciation of women actors in *Histriomastix* (1633) – published a month before the Queen herself performed in a masque – led to his conviction for sedition. Shirley, who was either a Catholic himself, like the Queen, or at very least an unusually outspoken Catholic sympathiser – denounced the Puritan Prynne in the mock-dedication to his play *The Bird in a Cage*, ironically praising his 'Love to *Learning, especially to that Musicall part of humane knowledge* Poetry'.[3] While the Prynne incident was deep in the past by the time Vaughan arrived in London c.1640, a second sedition charge in 1637 still haunted the public memory – Prynne was branded and had his ears cut off – and his triumphant return

---

3 James Shirley, *The Bird in a Cage: A Comedie* (London, 1633), sig A2r.

to London in late 1640, after the Long Parliament had recalled him from exile in the Channel Islands, stood as a clear demonstration that the religious tensions of the 1630s could not be banished forever.

Despite the return of Prynne and the growing political and religious tensions in London, Vaughan would have found the Inns of Court a congenial environment for an aspiring poet, and a place where forms of literary sociability were still very much on the agenda. One of the most important literary activities was the sharing and copying of poetry in manuscript miscellanies, with the Inns offering unrivalled access to verse from Oxford and Cambridge, as well as the poetry of law students and members of the Inns' literary circles. Shirley had certainly been circulating his lyric poetry within the Inns from at least the early 1630s, and manuscript evidence suggests that he also made efforts to re-circulate them after returning from Ireland in 1640. On one of the end leaves of Bodleian MS Rawl. poet. 88, the most important manuscript of Shirley's poems, copied *c*.1640–42, are the signatures of three lawyers, Andrew and Joseph Wall and Robert D'Oyley, who all became members of the Inns at almost exactly the same time Shirley moved to Holborn in 1627, a period in which he was busy making connections in London's literary world.[4]

Shirley's lyric poems (my edition of which is forthcoming from Oxford University Press) are now known even less than his plays, although small selections sometimes appear in anthologies.[5] Yet the poems number over a hundred, and were written throughout his career alongside the plays and entertainments, showing Shirley's mastery of a range of fashionable genres – lyrics of love and loss, songs, elegies and epitaphs, adaptations from classical literature, meditative verses. His *Poems &c.* (1646) is also interesting as one of the poetical outputs of the bookseller Humphrey Moseley, who the previous year had published Milton's *Poems*, and who would later publish Vaughan's *Olor Iscanus* (1651), *Flores Solitudinis* (1654)

---

[4] The manuscript contains additions by Shirley, who also copied out the final leaf of verse; see Peter Beal, *Catalogue of English Literary Manuscripts* (https://celm-ms.org.uk/introductions/ShirleyJames.html/).

[5] The most notable modern selection is that of *Seventeenth-Century British Poetry, 1603–1660*, ed. by John P. Rumrich and Greg Chaplin [New York: Norton, 2006]), with nine poems. The absence of a complete edition of Shirley since Alexander Gifford and James Dyce's *Works* (John Murray, 1833) is surely a significant factor in Shirley's neglect as both poet and playwright.

and *Hermetical Physick* (1655).[6] Whereas Vaughan's *Poems* announced a new poetic talent, Shirley (b. 1596) would turn 50 in the year his book appeared, giving it a retrospective cast, though – as with Robert Herrick's massive *Hesperides* (1648) – the act of looking back led to the creation of something new and forward-looking, notably in the way manuscript verse was rearranged and revised for print – as I discuss further below.

Naturally enough, direct critical comparisons of Vaughan and Shirley have been few. For reasons good and bad, both writers are generally compartmentalised in critical discussion – Shirley limited to his writing of comedy and tragicomedy, Vaughan to the devotional lyric – and of course both signal strong literary influences – to Jonson, Fletcher, and Webster; to Herbert – that demand precedence. One notable exception to the non-meeting of this twain are the brief contrasts in Jonathan Post's excellent monograph *Henry Vaughan: The Unfolding Vision*, where Shirley is instanced as an index of the 'light' cavalier style that, as Post argues, Vaughan rejected as he turned to devotional writing in the manner of Herbert. Adapting a metaphor from Shirley's poem 'Love for Enjoying', Post describes the Caroline poets as lapidaries, whose art was not meant to be original but to 'cut, polish, and refine what had already been made available to him by the tradition'.[7] Unlike Donne and Jonson, that is, the Carolines lacked a creative originality in style or substance, and were content to draw on their predecessors – for instance, Shirley twice draws on Donnean imagery in 'Love for Enjoying', at ll. 14 and 21 – without making their achievement new. In support of this view, one might quote Shirley's contemporaries, who praised him not for a Donnean 'line / Of masculine expression' (as Carew's praised Donne in his elegy), but for what they perceived as the sophisticated 'smoothness' of his lines.

Post's comparison holds well for Vaughan: his later, greater achievements clearly leave behind the style of *Poems*. But it is less satisfactory for helping us understand why Shirley wrote as he did, or why he was admired by contemporaries, or what he was trying to achieve in the printed *Poems &c.* in 1646. As I will suggest, Shirley was far from comfortable with the fashionable, courtly style

---

6 Shirley's *Poems &c.* was printed mostly by Ruth Raworth, whose shop had also produced Milton's, as well as Sir John Suckling's *Fragmenta Aurea* earlier in 1646.

7 Jonathan F. S. Post, *Henry Vaughan: The Unfolding Vision* (Princeton: Princeton University Press, 1982), p. 9.

of polish and glitter, and his plays often draw on such language as an index of pure hypocrisy or treachery in creating their vice characters and antagonists. So while Shirley inevitably wrote with one eye on fashionable court modes – as did Milton, even, or Marvell (who read Shirley with interest) – he usually wrote from a position of some critical detachment. It is of course true that he nurtured an ambition to win approval at court, and that he had his hopes dashed in 1638 when William Davenant, protégé of the courtier Thomas Carew, succeeded Jonson as Laureate.[8] Yet despite energetically dedicating his work to sundry aristocratic patrons throughout the 1630s, Shirley never really found a foothold at court and grew increasingly disenchanted with its values.[9] His panegyric to Elizabeth Butler, the Countess of Ormonde, written in 1639, offers outright criticism of 'court idolatry' and those whose eloquence in verse helps the unworthy to 'wear / Silk at the cost of flatt'ry… by painting a great lady's face / When she had done't before' (ll. 6–7, 9–10). Whoever Shirley's immediate target was here – and doubtless the new Laureate, Davenant, cannot have been far from his thoughts – these lines act as a cue for us to reassess the 'courtliness', polish, and involvement with Caroline poetics in Shirley's verse, and to avoid taking them at face value until their contexts have been more fully examined.

*

Vaughan may have discovered Shirley through the dramatist's friendship with William Habington, whose *Castara* has long been recognised as a model for moments in Vaughan's early verse. As Robert Wilcher observes in his account of Vaughan's poetic borrowings, Habington was an 'important reservoir of material for Vaughan in his secular poems', and it is likely that Vaughan owned either the second or third edition of *Castara* (first edition 1634, expanded in 1635 and 1640), to judge from a reference to the poem '*Castara*'s smiles' in his 'To the River Isca'; Vaughan's 'To my Ingenuous Friend, R. W.', placed first in *Poems*, also contains a clear reworking of the final stanza of Habington's 'To Castara'.[10] As well as Habington's in-

---

8 On the quarrel between Massinger, Shirley and other dramatists with Davenant and Carew, see Peter Beal, 'Massinger at Bay: Unpublished Verses in a War of the Theatres', *Yearbook of English Studies*, 10 (1980), 190–3.

9 On Shirley's search for patronage see Sandra Burner, *James Shirley: A Study of Literary Coteries and Patronage in Seventeenth-Century England* (Lanham: University Press of America, 1988).

10 Robert Wilcher, 'Henry Vaughan's Borrowings in the Secular Poems: Plagiarism, Imitation, Allusion', *Scintilla*, 17 (2013), p. 15.

genious love poetry, Vaughan would no doubt have been engaged by the forms of Caroline literary sociability on display in Habington's writing, as we can see from Vaughan's imitation of the manner in 'A Rhapsodie. Occasionally written upon a meeting with some of his friends at the Globe Taverne'. According to Kenneth Allott, Habington's editor, Shirley was 'probably Habington's closest literary friend in London', their relationship dating from at least 1630 when Habington wrote complimentary verses for the first editions of Shirley's plays *The Wedding* and *The Grateful Servant*.[11] It is also possible that the two men were co-religionists, though firm proof of Shirley's Catholicism has not been established; more certain is that the two men maintained their connection, and indeed they may even have known each other during the Civil War when both joined the royalist army.

If Vaughan did not know for sure that Shirley was the 'friend' addressed by Habington in 'To a Friend, inviting him to a meeting upon Promise', then he must have wondered who the friend was, since the poem is a reply to that friend's mock-accusation of betrayal. Shirley's poem 'To E. H. and W. H.' (as it is entitled in manuscript) might also have circulated in the 1630s; certainly Shirley included it in the scribal manuscript he had produced in the early 1640s (Bodleian, MS Rawl. poet. 88) and he also published it in 1646 with the title 'To Gentlemen that Broke Their Promise of a Meeting, Made When They Drank Claret'. Shirley's original version dates from c.1634, so may also have circulated in miscellany copies alongside Habington's poem, though if so none have survived. Though Habington's poem did not appear in the first edition of *Castara* (1633), his reply to Shirley contains scornful allusions to William Prynne – whom Shirley had baited in his mock-dedication to his *The Bird in a Cage* (1633) – suggesting a date of 1633 or early 1634. Inviting Shirley to partake of fine sack, Habington notes that 'Of this wine should Prynne / Drinke but a plenteous glasse, he would beginne / A health to Shakespeares ghost' (ll. 5–7). Both Habington's and Shirley's poems ring with similar scornful rejections of Puritan abstemiousness, and praise wine-drinking and oaths as a mark of loyalty to both king and poetry. Even though Shirley is writing a mock-rebuke at the forgetfulness of Habington (and the other, unknown friend), the poem acts to reaffirm the shared values and beliefs rather than actual censure.

---

11 *The Poems of William Habington*, ed. by Kenneth Allott (Liverpool: University of Liverpool Press, 1948), p. xxix. All quotations of Habington's poems are from this edition.

A knowing reader might well have connected Shirley and Habington through these poems, then, and especially one with access to the literary culture of the Inns of Court, not to mention the wider world of literary London. (As Roland Mathias suggested, Vaughan probably met Katherine Philips at the literary salon of her father, John Fowler, to which he could have been introduced by John Jeffreys of Abercynrig, a known member of 'this circle of literary cavaliers'.[12]) Since Habington's poems do not survive in many manuscript copies, it is difficult to establish his contemporary non-print readership, and such miscellanies as contain poems by *both* Habington and Shirley do not lend support to the idea that Vaughan would have read them side-by-side. One later seventeenth-century miscellany, Bodleian, MS Rawl. poet. 65, contains 19 of Habington's poems and also Shirley's song 'Strephon, Daphne' (sung in *The Cardinal*) but its date makes it of limited evidential use (though it is possible that it derives from an earlier collection). More interesting is British Library, Harley MS 3511, which dates from the mid-century, and contains not only 10 Habington poems (alongside 14 by Donne, 6 by Carew, and at least 13 by Randolph) but also Shirley's 'Would you know what's soft?' and 'Love's Hue and Cry'. However, again the evidence is of limited value, in this case because the owner and probable compiler of the manuscript, Arthur Capell, second Earl of Essex, derived his texts from printed books.[13] The fact that Capell thought these poems belonged together in his miscellany is interesting, of course, and his lack of attributions should remind us that early modern readers were frequently far more interested in the *poem* than they were the *poet*. Elsewhere in the manuscript record we also find songs by Shirley and Habington collected together in Bodleian, MS Don. c. 57, a book of songs compiled from the 1640s on, and which as well as a setting of 'Would you know what's soft?' included Habington's 'To Castara, Looking backe at her departing' and 'To Cvpid, Vpon a dimple in Castara's Cheeke'. (Again, though, a preponderance of Carew texts makes it possible that misattribution is again at work.) A final instance of Habington and Vaughan coinciding in a songbook is the composer John Gamble's songbook (now New York Public Library, Drexel MS 4257) which contains

---

12 See *Works*, vol. III, p. 1021.
13 Ironically, Capell's texts almost certainly derive from printed editions of *Carew*, where a number of poems by Shirley had appeared misattributed. Shirley's sardonic 'Postscript to the Reader' in *Poems &c.* reflects his awareness of the ironies attendant on manuscript transmission.

three Shirley songs ('wt should my Mistris doe wth: hayre', 'Hearke hearke how in euery groue', and 'Cupid calls com Louers com') and Habington's 'To Castara, Looking backe at her departing'. Taken as a whole, the manuscript record offers little firm evidence to suggest that someone like Vaughan, interested in Habington and with access to poetry in manuscript, would have found them in the same close company their poetry suggests they kept away from the page.

Of course, since Shirley's own poems were not published until 1646, Vaughan must have read them, if at all, in manuscript. The manuscript evidence that has survived suggests that Shirley's verse was commonly copied into three main kinds of miscellany compilations.[14] On the one hand, his dramatic songs were popular with London's musical and literary circles, and appear in the songbooks of composers such as John Gamble and William Lawes. Usually these are songs of love and beauty, a subject which finds Shirley usually steering just this side of tongue-in-cheek – as, for instance, in his popular song 'Would you know what's soft?', in which the mistress is said to excel snow in whiteness, honey in sweetness, and so on through the five senses, in a delightful imitation of Jonson's lyric 'Her Triumph'. Shirley's humour in his songs usually has a comic but serious dramatic purpose, as in the praise of ugliness in a song (set by William Lawes) later retitled 'One That Loved None but Deformed Women', but known in songbooks as 'What Should My Mistress Do With Hair?'. Within *The Duke's Mistress* the song forms part of the play's 'consciousness of the relevance of the theme [of deformity] to Platonic *préciosité*'.[15]

A second, more likely route by which Vaughan could have read Shirley is through manuscript copies of Shirley's lyrics that the poet himself circulated at the Inns of Court. A significant indication of what sorts of poetry was available is the professional scribal miscellany now known as the 'Chute' manuscript, a collection dating from *c.*1636 and which was owned by, and probably produced for, the lawyer and MP, Chaloner Chute, then living at The Vyne in Hampshire. As Arthur Marotti and others have discussed, the Chute manuscript contains a wide range of university, urban, and courtly

---

14 Omitted here is any discussion of the unique circulation patterns of some of Shirley's occasional poems, such as 'Upon the Prince's Birth' and the anti-Puritan satire beginning 'Cobblers and coopers and the rest', which are less relevant to the immediate contexts of discussion.
15 Peter Ure, 'The "Deformed Mistress" Theme and the Platonic Convention', *Notes and Queries*, 193 (1948), 269–70 (p. 270).

poetry dating from the 1620s and 30s, and 'reflects, as do many similar anthologies, not only the personal interests of the compiler, but also some of the shared interests of an early Stuart social and political elite living in a time of change and conflict'.[16] The book is also clearly marked by its Inns of Court origins, featuring a legal epigram, poems on drunk lawyers, and a poem about Shirley's *The Triumph of Peace*, the masque staged in 1634. In terms of Shirley's lyric poems, the Chute manuscript is notable for having the single greatest concentration of his poetry outside of the semi-autograph Bodleian, MS Rawl. poet. 88, with a total of 14 poems (plus a song from *The Triumph of Peace*). This unusual concentration suggests that the compiler had access to Inns of Court texts, in Shirley's case indicating a source fairly close to the writer himself; in other words, Chute provides our best sense of which texts Shirley chose to circulate, and thus what could have been available to a reader like Vaughan in the later 1630s or early 1640s. Notably, the first of the Shirley poems to appear in Chute, 'The Garden' – alluded to by Andrew Marvell in his more famous poem of that name – is one of the handful of poems by Shirley that textual evidence suggests Vaughan *might* have read, as I discuss below.

A final context for reading Shirley's poems in 1640s London was their inclusion in a group of manuscripts miscellanies that Margaret Crum first proposed were copied from the same archetype, probably separates available to borrow from a bookseller.[17] The five poems by Shirley to feature in this archetype are striking for their critical attitude to the Platonic love cult of the 1630s. As well as 'Love for Enjoying' (the poem discussed by Post, which was always known in manuscript as 'To His Mistress Whom He Loved To Enjoy') and the sensory delights of the song 'Would You Know What's Soft', these texts also include a poem in mock outrage at gentleman who 'Loved a Great Mistress and Durst Not Discover It'; a poem on 'The Courtesan'; and a corrective address 'To a Gentleman (That Magnified His Mistress) The Praise of a Maister' that ridicules hyperbolic mistress-worship. Whoever compiled the original archetype

---

16 See Arthur Marotti, 'Chaloner Chute's Poetical Anthology (British Library, Additional MS 33998) as a Cosmopolitan Collection', in *English Manuscript Studies 1100–1700, Volume 16: Manuscript Miscellanies c.1450–1700*, ed. by Richard Beadle and Colin Burrow (London: British Library, 2012), pp. 112–40 (p. 112).

17 Margaret Crum, 'An Unpublished Fragment of Verse by Herrick', *Review of English Studies*, 11 (1960), 186–89; see also the further identifications and discussion in Mary Hobbs, *Early Seventeenth-Century Verse Miscellany Manuscripts* (Aldershot: Scolar, 1992), pp. 124–9.

from which these manuscripts were copied evidently associated Shirley's poems with a sensuousness that amounts to a rejection of the purely spiritual love promoted by the Caroline cult of *préciosité*. Indeed, the very title of 'Love for Enjoying' 'improperly' connects actions that were supposed to be strictly kept apart – since, as Erica Veevers had noted, 'beauty and virtue may be *loved* by all, [but] individual beauties [were] to be *enjoyed* only in marriage'.[18] Although Shirley was not above writing a poem of intense admiration of a courtly mistress – for instance, in his aubade 'Good Morrow' – he was more widely known to poetry readers for reacting sceptically against the courtly love associated in the period with the married chastity of Charles and Henrietta Maria.

*

Vaughan's *Poems* (1646) takes no time in establishing its literary credentials: the opening lines 'To my Ingenious Friend, R. W.', allude to 'Great BEN' Jonson, and to his most famous 'son', Thomas Randolph, who (as the new Oxford edition reminds us) was a relation of the 'R. W.' of the title, whose acquaintance thus brings Vaughan a step closer to the literary greats.[19] The second and third poems further recall Randolph, imitate Habington, and use the same Petrarchan image of the mistress's breath as Carew's 'Prayer to the wind'. More hints of Randolph, Donne, and possibly Edward Herbert follow, before the reader finally arrives at 'To his Friend Being in Love', one of two poems which might suggest that Vaughan *had*, in fact, read poems by Shirley – specifically, one of the 'Crum' group of texts, almost always known in manuscript as 'One That Loved a Great Mistress and Durst Not Discover It'. In Vaughan's poem the speaker urges himself to tell his mistress of his love (the lines appear to address a second person, but are actually directed inwardly):

---

18 Erica Veevers, *Images of Love and Religion: Queen Henrietta Maria and Court Entertainments* (Cambridge: Cambridge University Press, 1989), p. 60 (my emphasis).
19 *Works*, vol. III, p. 842, citing the research of Louise Imogen Guiney.

> Aske Lover, ere thou dyest; let one poor breath
> Steale from thy lips, to tell her of thy Death;
> Doating Idolater! can silence bring
> Thy Saint propitious? or will *Cupid* fling
> One arrow for thy palenes? leave to trye
> This silent Courtship of a sickly eye. [...]
> Aske her, foole, aske her, if words cannot move,
> The language of thy teares may make her love.
> (ll. 1–6, 11–12)

Jonathan Post and others have remarked on this poem's similarity to Suckling's witty anti-Platonic 'Why so pale and wan fond Lover?', whose reference to the lover's pallor Vaughan certainly seems to have picked up alongside its theme of speechlessness:

> Why so dull and mute young Sinner?
> Prithee why so mute?
> Will, when speaking well can't win her
> Saying nothing doo't?
> Prithee why so mute?[20]

Suckling is a likely influence on Vaughan's poem, but 'speechless lover' poems were far from unusual: musical versions, for instance, included Thomas Wilson's song 'I love a lass but dare not show it' (pub. in Playford, *Select Musical Ayres* in 1652, but in manuscript much earlier) and ballads such as *A New Ditty of a Lover, Tost Hither and Thither, that Cannot Speake his mind When They are Together* (1640). A common poetic inspiration for all of these, including perhaps Suckling, may be Jonson's 'Celia' poems, and notably 'Drink to me only with your eyes' with its deft evocation of the language of eyes, looks, and silences.

Shirley's silent lover poem, known in the 'Crum' group copies as 'One That Loved a Great Mistress and Durst Not Discover It' constitutes another possible source for Vaughan's 'To his Friend'. As in Vaughan's poem (but not Suckling's), Shirley has his speaker address himself about his reticence to speak:

---

20 ll. 6–10, text from Suckling's *Aglaura* (1638), p. 23.

> I can no longer hold, my body grows
> Too narrow for my soul, sick with repose,
> My passions call to be abroad; and where
> Should I discharge their weight, but in her ear
> From whose fair eyes the burning arrow came,
> And made my heart the trophy to her flame?
> I dare not. How? Cupid is blind we know,
>
> I never heard that he was dumb till now;
> Love, and not tell thy mistress? How crept in
> That subtle shaft? Is it to love a sin?
> Is't ill to feed a longing in my blood?
> And was't no fault in her to be so good?
> I must not then be silent; yet forbear,
> Convey thy passion rather in some tear,
> Or let a sigh express, how much thy bliss
> Depends on her, or breathe it in a kiss,
> And mingle souls.
>
> (ll. 7–17)[21]

The similarities between these lines and Vaughan's are as striking, if not more so, than those between Vaughan's and Suckling's. Both Vaughan and Shirley write in first person, and both are self-accusations for inaction and cowardice. Their language and imagery are also akin, both drawing on Cupid and his wayward arrows, and on the idea that if the lover dare not speak, he might alternatively express his meaning through a physical language of emotion such as tears (Vaughan's 'language of thy tears' and Shirley's 'in some tear / Or … a sigh'; ll. 12; and 14–15). Of course, both Vaughan and Shirley may have each independently been imitating Jonson, or indeed even Suckling, although it is impossible to say whether Suckling's poem preceded Shirley's or vice versa. Additionally, however, there is what might be a further reminiscence of Shirley in Vaughan's speaker's vision of his tears falling on 'her breasts warmer snow', a line which appears remarkably close to one from Shirley's popular song 'Strephon, Daphne' – performed onstage in *The Cardinal* in November 1641 – in which Strephon tells his beloved that: 'In thy perfumed bosom then I'll stray, / In

---

21 All quotations from Shirley are from my forthcoming edition of the poems for Oxford University Press. In accordance with the textual policy of the *Complete Works* of which it is a part, spelling is lightly modernised.

such warm snow who would not lose his way?'. The origins of both images are Petrarch's *calda neve* (*Rime*, 157.9) but Shirley's song was a popular manuscript poem in the early 1640s – it would even prompt various travesties during the Civil War, such as 'Come, my Oliver' about the Lord Protector[22] – but the coincidence of phrasing, in a poet as verbally retentive as Vaughan, is certainly suggestive.

Another possible influence of Shirley on Vaughan comes in the final poem in the lyrical section of *Poems* (1646), 'Upon the Priorie Grove, His usuall Retyrement'. Parts of this lovely poem might, I suggest, constitute an imitation, or at least a reminiscence, of Shirley's poem 'The Garden', the lyric found on p. 27 of the Chute manuscript, and which was probably among circulating collections of Shirley's verse at the Inns of Court. In both poems, speakers praise a private garden space that represents a retreat from the world: the grove of Brecon Priory for Vaughan – the place where he wooed his first wife, Catherine Wise – and for Shirley's speaker a solitary garden which is variously named in early manuscripts as 'Chlorinda's Garden', 'Cardias Garden' and 'The Authors Garden', though in *Poems &c.* it is simply '*The* Garden'. If Vaughan read the poem in a copy from the late 1630s, it would have contained the following stanzas in which the speaker is describing how he would set out his melancholy garden retreat:

> 3. In the violet's drooping head
> Will my counterfeit appear,
> A little time, but witherèd;
> But no woodbine shall grow there.
>
> 4. Weave a pretty roof of willow,
> On each side let blackthorn grow,
> Raise a bank, where for my pillow
> Wormwood, rue, and poppy strow.
>
> 5. No bird sing here but Philomel
> Or the orphan turtle groan,
> Either of these two can tell
> My sad story, by their own.
>
> (ll. 9–20)

---

[22] See Adam Smyth, '*Profit and Delight*': *Printed Miscellanies in England, 1640–1682* (Detroit: Wayne State University Press), pp. 96–7.

Whether or not Vaughan was thinking specifically of these lines Shirley's when he wrote, 'Upon the Priorie Grove' offers a striking counterpoint to Shirley's speaker's vision:

> Henceforth no melancholy flight
> No sad wing, or hoarse bird of Night,
> Disturbe the Aire, no fatall throate
> Of Raven, or Owle, awake the Note
> Of our laid Eccho, no voice dwell
> Within these leaves, but *Philomel*.
> The poisonous Ivie here no more
> His false twists on the Oke shall score,
> Only the Woodbine here may twine,
> As th'Embleme of her Love and mine.
>
> (ll. 5–14)

Where Shirley's speaker dreams of the solitary life Marvell would later imagine in his own 'The Garden' (where 'Two paradises 'twere in one / To live in paradise alone'), free from visitors and from womankind, Vaughan evokes the place where he had the company of his future wife, Catherine Wise, so that 'Upon the Priory Grove' reads like an amorous, or even Edenic, reworking of Shirley's vision. Vaughan explicitly *allows* the growth of the woodbine, as an emblem of married love, that Shirley's speaker *prohibits* on the same grounds. Both speakers will permit only the song of the nightingale Philomel to be heard, but the meaning of her song contrasts sharply: Vaughan hears a song of love, but Shirley's speaker hears only a lament, perhaps suggesting a bitter experience of love, making the bird's a suitable voice to 'tell / My sad story, by their own' (ll. 19–20). Such details might amount to a creative imitation, or at least a memory of Shirley on Vaughan's part; if so, it may also be significant that while Vaughan welcomes the 'Amorous Sunne' and its sunbeams into the Grove, Shirley's poem opens with the speaker explicitly seeking a shady spot, a 'plot of land / Which the sun did never see' (ll. 1–2). No surprise, then, that he issues an outright ban on genial visitors, expelling 'wanton lover[s]' from his garden on all accounts (ll. 1–3).

Such verbal similarities as I have pointed out are of course far from suggesting a substantial influence. After all, if Vaughan had encountered some of Shirley's verse in the 'Crum' group, the poems are likely to have been unascribed, or even wrongly attributed to Carew or Randolph (though that would not mean that he could not have admired and borrowed from them). Even if the poems *were* ascribed, most collections to feature Shirley held only a handful of poems, usually no more than five, as in the 'Crum' group. And even if Vaughan, tracing back from Habington to Shirley, had sought out the latter's poetry through connections at the Inns of Court, he could probably only have found a collection of 14 poems, if we are to judge by the Chute manuscript. Any encounter, then, must have been fleeting. Nevertheless, as Wilcher has demonstrated, Vaughan's magpie brain could gather material from across his wide reading, and he would surely also have appreciated the lyrical qualities to be found in Shirley, whose stylistic 'smoothness' was prized by contemporary readers.[23]

*

To conclude, I want to return to the idea that Shirley's *Poems &c.* forms, in a different but related way to Vaughan's *Silex Scintillans*, a critical response to Caroline verse and to the events of the 1640s, and a search for a poetic renewal. Throughout his career as a dramatist Shirley had sought to reform the behaviour of the powerful, demonstrating the corruptions of power and status while exploiting the last-minute get-outs of the tragicomic genre to suggest that a turn to virtue could bring about stability and continuance among the foolish (or often vicious) aristocracy and gentry. From the late 1630s on, however, Shirley seems to have become increasingly doubtful that the court itself was really open to reform. Praising the Countess of Ormonde in 1639, for instance, he contrasted her 'chaste' and unadorned life and beauty with the exaggerations and paintings of the English court. 'Were you but only great', he writes to her,

---

23 Wilcher, 'Henry Vaughan's Borrowings'.

>   there are some men
> Whose heat is not the Muses', nor their pen
> Steered by chaste truth, could flatter you in prose,
> Or glorious verse, but I am none of those:
> I never learned that trick of court to wear
> Silk at the cost of flatt'ry, or make dear
> My pride, by painting a great lady's face
> When she had done't before, and swear the grace
> Was nature's; anagram upon her name,
> And add to her no virtue, my own shame.
> I could not make this lord a god, then try
> How to commit new court idolatry.
>   ('To the Excellent Pattern of Beauty and Virtue,
>   Lady E[lizabeth], Co[untess] of Or[monde], ll. 1–12)

In their dislike of 'glorious' poetry, these lines deride the showy, exaggerated verse that plays superficially and hyperbolically with words, seeking its own advantage, not that of the subject or reader. Shirley also hints, in 'glorious verse' at the superficiality of the Caroline court, with its taste for masques celebrating the 'triumph' of Charles and Henrietta Maria – something not earned through any particular achievements but rather through the 'glorious'-ness of their style and appearance. Against such superficial style, Shirley suggests that 'chaste truth' can still be embodied in poetry if the 'wit' consists not of self-ingenuity, but in the choice of worthy subjects to commemorate. (The influence of Ben Jonson's pantheon of the virtuous in *Epigrams* and *The Forest* is apparent here.) The poem goes on to offer very conspicuously conventional and unelaborate wishes: for happy married life, healthy children, long life, and a heavenly reward after death.

That Shirley extensively revised his poetry, probably in the aftermath of the first Civil War – is easily seen by comparing his earlier manuscript compilation, now Bodleian, Rawl. poet. 88 (copied *c.*1640–2) with the collection he printed four years later as *Poems &c.* The earlier, manuscript collection lacks a discernible order, and its texts are generally only lightly revised. *Poems &c.*, by contrast, undertakes an extensive renovation of Shirley's poetic oeuvre that amounted to a revisionary and critical representation of his previous twenty-five years of poetry. This revisionary and self-critical effort was clearly perceived by Shirley's youthful patron, Thomas Stanley (b. 1625), the poet and philosopher whose 'Order of the Black Riband', founded in 1646, signalled sympathy for the sufferings of

Charles I by the wearing of a black armband, and numbered Shirley, Sherburne, and other poets and writers (including probably Herrick) among its original members.[24] In his poem heading the commendatory verse prefaced to Shirley's *Poems &c.*, Stanley marvelled at his friend's ability both to embody and also to step back from the Caroline poetic manner to reveal its artifice. In this, Shirley is:

> like some skilful artist, that to wonder
> Framing a piece, displeased, takes it asunder,
> Thou beauty dost depose, her charms deny,
> And all the mystic chains of love untie;
> Thus thy diviner muse and power 'bove fate
> May boast, that can both make, and uncreate.
> (ll. 7–12)

In Stanley's analysis, Shirley's poetry holds the power both to frame and to unframe, to create and uncreate; he has mastered the language of love and beauty, but growing dissatisfied has chosen to 'depose' it, and in so doing rises above the power of fate itself. Stanley's analysis seems itself to be a knowing imitation of Thomas Carew's 'Ingratefull beauty threatned', in which the speaker warns Celia to desist from triumphing in her glory, 'Lest what I made, I *uncreate*' (l. 14, my emphasis).[25] Where Carew's speaker is locked antagonistically into a relationship with the mistress he has formerly praised, Shirley's antagonism is with love itself, and with its muse, the language of Platonic admiration and *préciosité* that came to dominate at court during the 1630s. Stanley goes on to see Shirley as restoring the literary arts, awarding him the laurel crown denied by Charles and Henrietta Maria in 1638:

> Thus into dying poetry, thy muse
> Doth full perfection and new life infuse,
> Each line deserves a laurel.
> (ll. 23–5)

---

24 Shirley's poem 'On a Black Riband' dates from 1646, and was published in *Poems &c*. On the 'Order of the Black Riband' see Nicholas McDowell, *Poetry and Allegiance in the English Civil Wars: Marvell and the Cause of Wit* (Oxford: Oxford University Press, 2008), pp. 13–52.

25 Text from *The Poems of Thomas Carew*, ed. by Rhodes Dunlap (Oxford: Clarendon Press, 1957).

Repaying the compliment, Shirley located in Stanley a figure whose charisma, virtue, and prodigious literary talent could direct English poetry towards a new lyrical style – one based on the achievements of Caroline verse, but purged of its ornamental excesses and hyperbole, the stylistic corollaries, as Shirley had come to feel, of self-interest and flattery. Directly comparing his protégé with Carew, Shirley praises Stanley's verse in terms that emphasise the link between poetic style and morality:

> Carew, whose numerous language did before
> Steer every genial soul, must be no more
> The oracle of love, and might he come
> But from his own to thy Elysium,
> He would repent his immortality
> Given by loose idolators, and die
> A tenant to these shades, and by thy ray
> He need not blush to court his Celia.
> Thy numbers carry height, yet clear, and terse,
> And innocent, as becomes the soul of verse:
> Poets from hence may add to their great name,
> And learn to strike from chastity a flame.
> ('To His Honoured Friend Thomas Stanley Esquire,
> upon His Elegant Poems', ll. 13–24)[26]

Stanley's writing is 'chaste' because it corrects the moral and aesthetic failings of the writers associated with the Caroline court – summed up for Shirley in the notorious sexual 'Elysium' (l. 16) of Carew's 'A Rapture' – but also informing the very language of poetry itself, with its tendency to inflation, hyperbole, and self-serving wit.

If Shirley's tribute to Stanley is perhaps the most overt piece of literary criticism in *Poems &c.*, it is certainly in the ordering and organisation of the volume as a whole that Shirley's expressed most clearly his critical response to Caroline literary culture. Just as Vaughan's *Silex Scintillans* begins with the speaker of 'Regeneration' becoming aware that his 'high-spring' is '[m]eere stage, and show' (l. 10), so too Shirley's book opens with the deceptive joys of lovers in springtime, as Cupid culls his 'wanton harvest' of virgins 'dandl[ing] on their stalk' to the fashionable pleasures of London's public

---

26 Shirley wrote this poem for Stanley's *Poems and Translations*, but due to a delay in that book's printing it actually appeared first in his own *Poems &c.*

gardens ('Cupid's Call', ll. 2, 7–8). This opening poem, 'Cupid's Call', is found only in *Poems &c.*, having been assembled by Shirley from two distinct songs of the 1630s, so that the book would open with this apparently triumphant vision of Caroline lyrical love. Its exaltation of Cupid is not without moments of proleptic strangeness – a harvest that is reaped in spring might give pause, for instance – but such problems are lost in the atmosphere of festivity and *carpe diem*. Cupid and his arrows continue to reign over the book's first two dozen poems: 'Love's Hue and Cry' evokes a comic chase after the mischievous God (playing on Moschus's first *Idyll*), while the speaker sends earnest pleas of love to 'Odelia', a mistress recalling Jonson's or Carew's 'Celia', or Habington's 'Castara'. Shirley even ventures to praise one courtly mistress in terms which unambiguously elevate her to the heavens: she 'Shoot[s] … from her silver brow more light / Then Cynthia, upon whose state / All other servile stars of beauty wait' ('Good Morrow', ll. 2–4).[27]

However, the joys of youthful love come to a sudden halt on page 28, as the book unceremoniously abandons Cupid for the image of a different royal child – the future Charles II. Shirley's festive celebration of the birth of Prince Charles in 1630, 'Upon the Prince's Birth', focuses on the loyal reaction of toasts and bonfires that greeted the birth of an heir to the throne in England, Scotland, Ireland and Wales, with France and the Netherlands cheering on for good measure. In 1646, the year Prince Charles had escaped England to go into exile in France, the poem would have acted as a rallying cry for those loyal to the crown, and an anticipatory expression of joy at his return. (In 1660 Shirley would write his *Ode upon the Happy Return of King Charles II*, pointedly using the same metre as his nativity poem of thirty years previous.) If Charles's return represents the future political renewal of the English nation, the next poem in *Poems &c.* embodies the rebirth of English *poetry* in a time of Civil War: this is his previously discussed panegyric 'To His Honoured Friend Thomas Stanley Esquire, upon His Elegant Poems'. Together, Shirley's two poems of rebirth, to Charles and to Stanley, dismiss the rule of Cupid and the past, setting the scene for the rest of the volume, which will replace the snares of love with the virtues of present loyalty and steadfastness. Subsequent poems celebrate Shirley's Irish patron, the Earl of Strafford, whose attainder and execution by Parliament in 1641 was a royalist *cause célèbre*. Strafford is joined

---

27 If the subject of this poem is Lucy Hay, Countess of Carlisle (as I suggest in my edition) then her heavenly eminence itself constitutes an indirect snub to Queen Henrietta Maria, frequently compared to Cynthia.

by other exemplary figures: the Countess of Ormonde, who embodies the chaste virtues lacking in the English court; the 'Honourable Lady D[orothy] C[urson]' (née Tufton), a Catholic patron of Shirley's whose constancy and devotion he celebrated by updating the poem he had first written to her and her sisters as far back as 1618[28]; a second poem about Strafford, celebrating his recovery from illness in 1640 (and pointedly avoiding elegising him, thereby staging another imagined scene of a loyal subject recovering); praise of Shirley's patron and commander in the royalist army, the Earl of Newcastle; and a touching poem on his friend Philip Massinger, whose life and verse are seen as inextricably virtuous. Of the elegies that follow, many remember the royalist war dead, and a significant number pay tribute to prominent Catholics.

At this point in the book, having set out his pantheon of the worthy and seemingly banishing Cupid forever, Shirley unexpectedly recalls the boy-god; but not this time to dramatize his power, but in order that he can meet his fate. The poem 'Cupid Ungodded' is found nowhere else in Shirley's oeuvre, so was probably written specifically for *Poems &c.*, or at least as a tribute to his new patron in the year of its publication, Thomas Stanley, whose interest in the Greek Anacreontea is reflected in their incorporation by Shirley into his poem. The effect of the poem is to recover Cupid from the neglect into which the book abruptly threw his some 45 pages earlier, only then to ceremoniously strip him of his power: his wings, arrows, bow, and belt are taken away one by one, before Cupid is sent packing, with a final explanation of his punishment:

> Know, wretch, thou shalt not die, before
> I see thee begging at each door;
> And taken for a vagrant stripped,
> Then by a furious beadle whipped,
> No more with roses, but with thorn:
> To all the word thus made a scorn.
> I'll give thee eyes before we part,
> To see thy shame, and break thy heart.
> (ll. 43–50)

This formal banishment is surrounded, within *Poems &c.* by a series of poems in which the power of love is continually displaced. As we have seen, the speaker of 'The Garden' (p. 69) vows never to

---

28 On this poem see my 'Editing James Shirley's Poems', *Studies in English Literature 1550–1900*, 52 (2012), 101–16.

admit women to his paradise; in 'Curse' (p. 71) the speaker issues his ill-wishes on the woman who has betrayed him, and a 'Proud Mistress' is 'jeered ... into dead and rotten' (p. 72). 'Fie on Love' ridicules all lovers, men and women, branding them as mad, and promising that marriage will only guarantee to make their fate 'ten times worse' (p. 75; l. 8); and the addressee of the penultimate poem, 'To a Beautiful Lady', is assured that beauty and honesty can never coexist. The final poem, 'Dialogue', tells an anonymous lover to 'Collect thy scattered sense' and 'Reduce [women] to their flesh and blood', or in other words to forswear the sort of poetic hyperbole that compares the mistress's neck to a 'throne', or to 'doves billing', and in so doing transforms a woman into a monster (ll. 36, 39, 34–5).

By the end of *Poems &c.*, then, the reader has been transported from 'love's spring garden' ('Cupid's Call', l. 1), through a pantheon of the virtuous, to the solitude of 'The Garden', to witness a vision of the banishment of love, and the abuse of truth and language it engenders. Though not the pilgrim's way trodden by the regenerate Vaughan of *Silex Scintillans*, it is nonetheless a path that leads determinedly away from the Caroline past, while acknowledging its own origins; and it is one which, alongside Shirley's extensive revisions, reshapes his poetry to speak to the literary present of late 1646, when the future of Charles, and of the three kingdoms, lay in doubt, as did the future course of English poetry.[29] Before 1647 was out, Thomas Stanley would follow Shirley's path when he published his translation of Ausonius's poem 'Cupid Crucified' in the delayed *Poems and Translations* (the book for which Shirley wrote his encomium on Stanley, heralding his 'chaste' style as the future of English verse). He could not have known that Henry Vaughan, too, was at work on a translation of Ausonius, or that, as Paul Davis has argued, 'there are a number of reasons to suspect' that Vaughan's reading of Ausonius was 'crucial to [his] spiritual development'.[30] It remains, though, a further striking and unexpected connection between Shirley and Vaughan, two poets whose reflections on poetry are less unlike than might at first appear.

---

29 Shirley's revisions to his poems are too extensive to discuss here, but see my article 'Editing James Shirley' (above) and my forthcoming edition, which is some instances will provide multiple texts where collation is rendered impractical (and indeed impossible) by the extent of Shirley's changes.

30 Paul Davis, *Translation and the Poet's Life* (Oxford: Oxford University Press, 2008), p. 65.

Pentre Ifan, Megalithic Burial Chamber, Nevern, Pembrokeshire
by David Brown

PATRICK DEELEY

The Absence

Then after all I was a ghost caught
in the glum light of morning,
gone from myself as I stepped closer
to what you could neither see

nor hear – the shingly click and rattle
behind our resident robin's song.
Or maybe he was calling out
my knack for getting things wrong –

the absence I felt applied
even to garden shrub and rockery;
my unawareness of you
except for some inkling of your hand

begun to wave, your voice an echo,
but my suited state now
was to be hushed, ethereal, and I took
the robin's note as disapproval

of the hurricane promised to hit
by afternoon. Without intent, I passed
through the adjacent wall
of the bank, its stainless-steel vault,

through the driver of a car
dusting up the street beyond, and for
one topsy-turvy moment
I seemed party to the lovely mess

of living, the liberty of its constraints,
still able to catch the drift
of clouds from the west, the swollen air
inclined not to floor me but to lift.

CLAIRE SCOTT

That Day in Hades

Because her stiletto heels were being worn down
and Jimmy Choo shoes are hard to find in this place
because she was tired of glamming up each day
a face full of make up, overpriced perfume
trying to please the demanding director
who eyes her shadowy bosom and wide hips
because she never gets any lines in this god-forsaken play
because she was tired of trusting
a lyre-playing boy who never listens, not once
who loses faith every time and turns and looks
(she has begged for his understudy to play the part)
because she was sick of being a shade
never getting to see the light
never returning to the world she loves
    a patch of sun, please
    a flash of purple sky
longing for Big Macs and Dunkin' Donuts
longing for champagne and soft silk blouses
that day Eurydice called in sick

Wings

A moving, stirring, almost fluttering
feeling in my scapulae
a something that is trying to happen
an almost wanting to rise
without the drag of this heavy body
this earthbound, leg-walking, plod-along body
a vague memory of soaring over fields
drifting through clouds
riding the glory of the wind
on great feathered wings
useless now, withered nubs, vestigial
like our tail bone, wisdom teeth and appendix
yet the longing lasts
we watch condors and eagles sail from cliffs
we watch finches at our feeder, touching
down, nibbling seeds, then flying free
we lower our heads to our morning toast and tea

CHRISTOPHER NORRIS

As Knowing Goes

for Valerie Norris

We know so many things, as knowing goes.
We know each dawn will bring
A symphony of birdsong, why
They're tuning up to sing
A chant that grows
More clamorous as Spring
Returns, and why it fills the sky,
That restless carolling
Whose explanation every knower knows.

It's scientific lights we know them by,
These wonders we suppose
Must finally, like everything,
Be destined to disclose
What prompts that cry,
That keep-off call to foes,
Or mating-song, or tune to fling
Out wide and silence those
Loud conspecifics giving theirs a try.

Amongst things that elude such reckoning
Are bird-songs that defy,
Once heard, all bids to make plain prose
Of poetry, and shy
From honouring
Song-contracts that apply
Alike to nightingales and crows
Since framed to keep alerts set high
Lest songbirds too melodiously take wing.

We've slept through their awakening, and it shows.
That's why our senses cling
To broken scraps of song that tie
Us to the ding-a-ling
Of tweets and close
Our ears to the bright ring
Of a dawn-chorus primed to fly
Beyond the harkening
Of souls attuned to mundane ratios.

AMANDA ATTFIELD

Exodus

Clouds poured across the carbon-loaded sky
and all things living fell before them. My feet
touched red sand, red water, the tide ran out

a long way and never came back, and my mother's voice
"*this too will pass…*". Nearby in the Service Station,
abandoned generators were silent, and distant wind

turbines turned and hummed to themselves.
I didn't want to you to wake me. Asleep,
I was the girl on the shingle waiting to step in,

I was the moon in the river, salmon swam through me,
I was a sail beyond the horizon. Awake, I was a swallow
dead in its nest, forked tail skyward. You'd wanted me

to stay, but I'd already gone. It may have been the rockets.
I was a broken arch leaning to find strength. I didn't want
this red-blooded dawn, silting my veins. No one could

explain the killing red rain, the sudden rain, the no rain
We were all busy at the fringes, moving apart, pruning
ourselves back to our roots. I remembered blue.

Flash of kingfisher, quarry of cobalt seawater
and pale faces pulled down, drowned in thick, dark air.
I'd walked away from bronze and iron tracks, their ruins

blew through me. I felt their call, and didn't reply.

Looking West at Birches Farm

Under the waxy, six hundred year old oak was shelter,
long grass bowed in its wake, a corn-coloured sea
with islands of red, and warblers sang in the hedgerow.
The ancient boundary road pulled like a magnet,
to smoke circles, ridge and furrow. Buttercups in the meadow,
were a tidal rush to the deep-trodden cut of the trackway.

Dark green and quiet, winding, unwinding, the trackway
was a sea-snake, muscular, and strong. Hidden in leaf shelter,
it moved with silent ease through the ocean meadow
over and on, back and further back to another kind of sea
ridden by blue-grey, whale-back mountains. What magnet
dragged them from water to high above land, and hedgerow

followed, land furrowed, filled and emptied. Hedgerow
sprang from fences and gullies along the trackway,
and you in your garden pruning, pruning, what magnet
made you prune clouds to neat circles, what kind of shelter
would interrupt you, stop you draining and ironing the sea
to settle here, on what it could become, this meadow,

left, or nearly left, to mind its own business. This meadow,
now, would you march it across the valley, stitch neat hedgerow
into that other time, repaint a perfect blue, pristine shallow sea,
where marine life swarmed along a Silurian trackway
to find food, migrate, become more, to take rest and shelter.
West had always been that setting sun, a last ray magnet

with its warm, end of day touch. Now no west-born magnet
will bring them back, those small sea creatures, their meadow
become mudstone, limestone their coffin, clay their tomb-shelter,
sandstone their graveyard, grown over by crops and hedgerow.
That wide ocean rose, silted all before it, before any trackway,
but there are seagulls here, though we are nowhere near the sea,

and buzzards and red kites, descendants of those who rode sea
breezes before any human breathed on earth. The magnet
of west, of moving and making, the drive onward, made the trackway,
miles trod over and over, weaving together mountains and meadow,
simple movement and sensible ways, fields and hedgerow,
oak, holly and hazel, birdsfoot and bugle, together they found shelter.

From the west, the strong sea breeze was a wrecker, no shelter
from carbon-black magnetic torrents that would suck up hedgerow,
sweep away both wild and unwild, bury trackway, and meadow.

SUSAN WALLACE

Earth Work

The nation's got the big house now; the far fields
gone, estate closed down. Last gardener to leave puts up his spade
with others hanging long to short like organ pipes; lays fork
across worn knees, rubs oiled rag on tines,
to conjure the last shine. With hooked thumbs hauls up braces,
left then right; pulls on his own, less sturdy boots,
draws laces tight. Checks all is as it should be.

The rosettes on the chimney breast –
Marrows, French Beans, Best in Show.
The leather harness strung up by the door.
Plant pots washed and stacked. Fire put out.
The horse-drawn roller, cobwebbed and cornered,
will outstay him, though it crushed a lad's leg once,
and him come through the trenches whole and hale.

Across two generations and a rope restraint
we pay to view his world, or what is left.
On the far wall small drawers spell out
the accumulated purpose of his days:
Peas, Radish, Celery, Beet (perpetual) –
seeds neatly named and stored,
waiting in the dark for a far season's sowing.

Beached

I walk the North Sea's edge, sandals in hand;
to my right the drowned plains of Doggerland.
To my left a friend, barely there, regales the wind
with her tale of how love has failed,
I barely listening, picturing instead stumps
of sunk forest, salted mammoths' bones,
as sea-dumped shells crunch like salt
under my soles. And then I see it:
child-sized and grey, rocking in the shallows.

Perfect in every part, fat and glistening
wet as a newborn, a dolphin's child,
washed up, waterlogged; its skin under my hands
smooth and human as a hairless head.
A passing stranger splashes in, heedless of his brogues.
Together we press and lift, press and lift,
coaxing heart and lungs to stutter and start.
It is inert as wet sand in a sack.
We can only send it back, to sink at sea.

My friend is facing landward, lost
in her monologue. Dazed by the drowning, I watch
the waves. And later, when I speak of it, she asks:
What dolphin?
I judged her then, resolved to see her less
while the sea rolled small bones to rest
in Doggerland. How did I fail to fathom
her heart's fierce need for succour,
stranded as she was in her life's shallows?

GRAHAM HIGH

Tilting at Windmills

They're harnessing the wind where the horses ran.
The turbine's slow semaphore is set to unhinge
our shielded sight where it dices up the sun.
We try to adapt: accept this silhouette of change.

A monument on highest ground, it juts
up like a menhir and bounds the old bucolic light
that lies forgotten here. Infrasonic, the bats
shun it; shift their eon-long stir of night.

And it's a lookout for the wind: a deity.
It's bladed trinity proclaims its love and pride
of power-industries and money. The moiety
of its divisions the warring nations will decide.

It needs its back-up, this gale-submitting tower.
We too are prone to pressure's vectors and
the unsecured, glib promises of easy power:
the partisan sectors that seek to bully the land

and its livings. But still, it has its beauty,
this slow-soar raptor, unbird-like in its fixity.
What gifts have we brought it? Only a duty
of care, a poem and, in our backpack, a picnic.

We try to lie like lovers under its span
and wonder if earth can meet the means, somehow,
of maintenance? Sometimes we hold hands
when we feel uncertain. We do so now.

Green Man

Pipes and tubing. His face is a foliate mask
of some earth archetype, seemingly asleep,
nose and mouth invaded; trailing out.

Strands and creepers. The earth, too,
is a life-support machine, of a sort,
which he has left, and has not left.

This is our son at his final hour of life.
Induced breath disturbs the flatness of
the bedsheet: disturbance, disturbance.

And all the time the tick and hum
of apparatus and the flicker of screens
around him and over him, and us in a ring

like a renaissance adoration scene.
We look at him as mute as if he were
some broken, carved pietà, still as stone.

Save for the movement of fluids and gases,
the subliminal, small bubbles and gurgles
waiting for the arbitrary word of 'now'.

We're stunned under the permeating weight,
the twines and tendrils of dawning collective
necessity towards that final unnatural decision.

And what's to distinguish, from the aqueous
cannulas, what is support and what seeks support
among the shoots and snags of feeling;

what feeds and what tears away at our
stems and roots? Here he is, all passion still,
whose love will ravel us forever.

GREG MILLER

Scythe

I walk across an open field
near monarch butterflies, milkweed,
and Queen Anne's lace. Solitary
together, free with you, whom I
may never see, hope's my meadow
that I must cut down into now.

Hope's not a post to lay a fence
from old rows down miraculous
turns, no ultimate enclosure,
acres staked, peopled with good sheep.
How much harm can one man do?
I am forever muddling through.

Metaphors lie. Stagnant cow pond,
smoked horizons, paralysis,
charm, and silence. Hoping amiss
for this or that, see: the whole lot
shifts, gets worse, or more like before:
quarantine, despots, hunger, war,

collapse, perhaps, of this green world
with all God's works. Best put to rest
the goat's torso, the lion's maw,
the fabulous Chimera's tale:
*Though held by a thread over hell
all manner of thing shall be well.*

All things we embrace fall apart,
desire's fire and faithful love,
the mighty along with the frail,
all fail, everything terrible
and true cutting me cutting through
woe's weeds, past the bitter-gold rue.

Henry Vaughan's Use of Biblical Epigraphs in Silex Scintillans

ROBERT WILCHER

I

It was not until the middle of the twentieth century that critics began to explore the significance of the Scriptures for an understanding of Henry Vaughan's devotional poetry. In 1950, M.M. Mahood was among the first to recognize that no other poet of his time had 'a more intimate knowledge of the Bible' than Vaughan.[1] Ten years later, E.C. Pettet devoted a chapter of his study of *Silex Scintillans* to illustrating the variety of ways in which Vaughan was indebted to the Scriptures – for subjects, images, phrases, and allusions.[2] And by the 1970s, the need for 'Biblical literacy' on the part of competent readers of Vaughan was widely acknowledged.[3] An important tool for further inquiry into the role of the Bible in Vaughan's poetry was furnished by Alan Rudrum's Penguin edition of 1976, which identified hundreds of sources in the Old and New Testaments. Rudrum's crucial insight was that 'serious reading of Vaughan involves an awareness of *how he employed* his biblical sources' (italics added).[4] This bore abundant fruit in Philip West's book-length demonstration

---

1 M.M. Mahood, *Poetry and Humanism* (London: Jonathan Cape, 1950), p. 255.

2 E.C. Pettet, *Of Paradise and Light: A Study of Vaughan's Silex Scintillans* (Cambridge: Cambridge University Press, 1960), pp. 32–50.

3 The phrase is from Robert Duvall's essay, 'The Biblical Character of Henry Vaughan's *Silex Scintillans*', *Pacific Coast Philology*, 6 (1971), 14. See also James Dale, 'Biblical Allusions in Vaughan's "The World"', *English Studies*, 51 (1970), 336–9; Eluned Brown, 'Vaughan's Biblical Landscapes', *Essays & Studies*, n.s. 30 (1977), 50–60; Kenneth Friedenreich's section about 'The Bible' in his chapter on 'Important Characteristics of Vaughan's Style' in *Henry Vaughan*, Twayne's English Authors Series (Boston: G.K. Hall, 1978), pp. 34–8.

4 *Henry Vaughan: The Complete Poems*, ed. Alan Rudrum (Harmondsworth: Penguin Books, 1976, revised 1983), p. 18.

that 'Vaughan's scripturalism' needs to be considered 'in the light of the scripture-using culture of the 1650s'.[5] A good deal has now been written about Vaughan's uses of biblical tropes, language, typology, and allusions, but a matter that has not received more than passing attention is his practice of attaching biblical epigraphs to many of his poems. Pettet distinguishes between poems 'in which an accompanying Biblical text merely provides some relevant quotation' and such poems as 'Isaacs Marriage' and 'Mans Fall, and Recovery', which read 'like intent cogitations on some Scriptural incident or text'; Barbara Lewalski argues that an epigraph serves a more integrated function as 'a biblical frame for the spiritual experience the poems explore'.[6] This paper will examine the different functions of epigraphs and the contribution they make to the reading of the poems they are attached to.

II

Sometimes an epigraph from Scripture (whether printed before or after a text) is little more than a sign that the poem is a meditation on the incident it records or the doctrine it formulates. For example, 'Isaacs Marriage' is introduced by a verse from the narrative of the patriarch's courtship of Rebekah in Genesis (24:63); and the epigraph to 'The Daughter of Herodias' directs the reader to the story – told in St Matthew's Gospel (14:3–11) – of Herod's adultery with his brother's wife and the dance by her daughter that led to the beheading of John the Baptist, all the details of which inform the final couplet: 'Thy mothers nets in thee were spred, / She tempts to *Incest*, thou to *blood*.'[7] The opening line of 'Buriall' – 'O Thou! the first fruits of the dead' – alludes to the passage from the First Letter to the Corinthians that was read out during the Prayer Book's burial service.[8] At the end of this poem, which Noel Thomas describes as 'deeply Pauline' in 'thought and image', Vaughan prints a verse from the Letter to the Romans that encapsulates the New Testament

---

5 Philip West, *Henry Vaughan's Silex Scintillans: Scripture Uses* (Oxford: Oxford University Press, 2001), p. 3.

6 Pettet, *Of Paradise and Light*, p. 32; Barbara Kiefer Lewalski, *Protestant Poetics and the Seventeenth-Century Religious Lyric* (Princeton NJ: Princeton University Press, 1979), p. 323.

7 *The Works of Henry Vaughan*, ed. Donald R. Dickson, Alan Rudrum, Robert Wilcher, 3 vols. (Oxford: Oxford University Press, 2018), pp. 68; 590. Hereafter cited as *HV Works*.

8 *HV Works*, p. 90.

doctrine of corporeal resurrection: '*And not only they, but our selves also, which have the first fruits of the spirit, even wee our selves grone within our selves, waiting for the adoption, to wit, the redemption of our body*' (Romans 8:23).[9] An even more striking illustration of Vaughan's dependence on the doctrinal authority of the Bible is the use of another verse from the same chapter of Romans (8:19) as a headnote for one of the untitled poems. The quotation from Beza's Latin translation of the epistle – '*Etenim res Creatæ exerto Capite observantes expectant revelationem Filiorum Dei*' [For the creatures, watching with lifted head, wait for the revelation of the sons of God] – is taken up directly in the first lines of the poem that follows as a welcome confirmation of beliefs held intuitively:

> And do they so? have they a Sense
> Of ought but Influence?
> Can they their heads lift, and expect,
> And grone too? why th'Elect
> Can do no more: my volumes sed
> They were all dull, and dead.[10]

Vaughan's preference for Beza's Latin here turns upon the phrase *exerto Capite* [with lifted head], which introduces a detail that does not appear in either of the English translations upon which he usually draws: 'For the earnest expectation of the creature waiteth for the manifestation of the sons of God' (King James or Authorised Version); 'For the feruent desire of the creature waiteth when the sonnes of God shalbe reueiled' (Geneva Bible). As Rudrum has shown, Beza's image plunges the poem into a theological debate about the status of animals in the divine scheme of things that had a long history in Christian controversy and had broken out with renewed vigour in the middle of the seventeenth century.[11] Vaughan's belief that the coming restoration is anticipated by the entire created world is reinforced by the verbs 'expect' and 'grone', the latter deriving from another verse in the same passage from Romans, translated in the Authorised Version as 'we know that the whole creation

---

9 See Noel Kennedy Thomas, *Henry Vaughan: Poet of Revelation* (Worthing: Churchman Publishing, 1986), p. 148.
10 *HV Works*, p. 95.
11 See Alan Rudrum, 'Henry Vaughan, the Liberation of the Creatures, and Seventeenth-Century English Calvinism', *The Seventeenth Century*, 4 (1989), 33–54.

groaneth and travaileth in pain together until now' (8:22).[12] This poem is not the only one for which Vaughan appears to have selected a particular version of the Scriptures to suit his poetic or doctrinal purpose. In order to provoke the exclamation that launches his meditation on Isaac's marriage – 'Praying! and to be married?' – and also to justify his later conceit of the young patriarch's soul taking flight towards God in the 'incense' of prayer, he substitutes 'pray' from the Geneva Bible for 'meditate' in a headnote otherwise taken word-for-word from the King James translation of Genesis (24:63): '*And Isaac went out to pray in the field at the Even-tide, and he lift up his eyes, and saw, and behold, the Camels were coming.*'[13] Indeed, West points out that he supplemented the Authorised Version of 1611, from which he took 'an overwhelming majority' of his biblical citations, not only with the English translation produced by Protestant exiles in Geneva during the reign of the Catholic Queen Mary and Beza's Latin New Testament, but also with the Roman Vulgate, the Protestant Latin bible of Junius-Tremellius, and Miles Coverdale's 1535 version of the Psalms in the Book of Common Prayer.[14]

First published in 1560 and frequently reprinted up to 1644, the Geneva Bible was the first to divide chapters into numbered verses for ease of reference. Since it was intended primarily for private study rather than liturgical use, it contained extensive marginal notes (often of a radical kind) to aid the lay reader. For several generations, it was the version preferred by Puritans, even after the 1611 translation had been authorized by the king for reading in services of the Church of England. As we shall see, four of the epigraphs to poems in the 1650 *Silex Scintillans* are from the Geneva Bible and three more (including the headnote to 'Isaacs Marriage') have a composite wording from the Geneva and the 1611 versions. This raises the question of why Vaughan chose to quote from the Geneva rather than the King James translation in four cases where the difference in wording has no obvious bearing on the text of the related poem.[15] The answer perhaps lies in the supreme authority vested in the Scriptures by the Protestant reformers of the sixteenth

---

12 Geneva also contains the verb 'groneth'.
13 *HV Works*, pp. 68–70.
14 See West, *Scripture Uses*, pp. 19–20.
15 See the headnote to 'Resurrection and Immortality' and the postscripts to 'Day of Judgement', 'Religion' and 'Disorder and frailty', *HV Works*, pp. 60, 64, 65, 110.

century, which was confirmed by the sixth of the Thirty-nine Articles appended to the Book of Common Prayer:

> Holy Scriptures containeth all things necessary to salvation: so that whatsoever is not read therein, nor may be proved thereby, is not to be required of any man, that it should be believed as an article of the faith, or be thought requisite or necessary to salvation.[16]

For an ardent – and scholarly – seeker after truth like Vaughan, the existence of alternative versions of the Bible in more than one language must have presented a difficulty. But since, as West explains, he believed that 'all readers, as long as they had the Holy Spirit as their guide, could understand and interpret it correctly', he would also have been sure that he was being led towards a translation that adequately expressed the divine intention.[17] Hence his delighted exclamation when he comes across Beza's Latin version of Romans 8:19: 'And do they so!'

Further problems arose, however, when Puritans who shared his trust in the guidance of the Holy Spirit arrived at interpretations that were antagonistic to his own beliefs. In the preface to the 1655 *Silex Scintillans*, he condemns 'Certain Authors' for being 'so irreverendly bold, as to dash *Scriptures*, and the *sacred Relatives* of *God* with their impious conceits'; and in 'White Sunday', he warns against those who lay claim to the same 'Prophetic fire' in interpreting the Word of God that had descended upon the Apostles at Pentecost:

> Though then some boast that fire each day,
> And on Christs coat pin all their shreds;
> Not sparing openly to say,
> His candle shines upon their heads.[18]

West observes that Vaughan goes out of his way to re-appropriate passages used frequently by his enemies for their own religious and political purposes. In 'Ascension-day', for example, he 'brings together prophecies from Malachi, Luke's gospel, Revelation and Acts' in support of his own anti-radical position. West's conclusion

---

16 *The Book of Common Prayer: The Texts of 1549, 1559, and 1662*, ed. Brian Cummings (Oxford: Oxford University Press, 2011), p. 675.
17 See West, *Scripture Uses*, p. 11.
18 *HV Works*, pp. 557, 569.

is that Vaughan could be 'every bit as partisan in his readings' as his opponents and 'every bit as convinced by what he read'.[19] This is the context in which he sometimes chose epigraphs from the Geneva translation favoured by Puritan polemicists, perhaps as a way of affirming that its wilful misuse by some readers did not mean that, in the right hands, it was any less authentic than the King James Bible or other available translations. Furthermore, his practice of quoting his epigraphs from a range of Latin and English translations indicates an awareness that both caution and discernment were necessary in searching out an acceptable version of the divinely inspired original.

III

Jonathan Post's explanation for Vaughan's use of biblical epigraphs is that the 'sizeable inscriptions from the Bible' at the end of some poems – he mentions 'Regeneration', 'Religion', 'The Brittish Church', 'The World', and 'The Mutinie' – 'sometimes verify and at other times correct the speaker's attitude; but in either case they deliver an intervening voice that seals off the poem on a gnomic note of authority'.[20] His need for external authorization or for confirmation of his spiritual insights and experiences is particularly evident in the sequence of poems with which he launched the new phase of his poetic career inaugurated by 'Regeneration' at the start of the 1650 *Silex Scintillans*. Each of the nine poems that follow this declaration of a new beginning is accompanied by a verse or two from the Scriptures, as if he felt that his own words needed corroboration from the Word of God or perhaps that publication demanded evidence of his religious credentials at the outset. John Wall argues that the widespread mediation of the Scriptures through the services of the Book of Common Prayer had been lost when its use was banned in the 1640s. The very title of 'Regeneration' was one of the words that were open to new definitions once they had been 'cut loose from their liturgical context'; and the poem itself charts a journey across 'a problematic landscape' full of bewildering symbolic features at which the speaker 'wonder'd much' without arriving at any certainty as to their meaning. Wall concludes that the pilgrim's experience in this poem is one of disorientation. The epigraph from

---

19 West, *Scripture Uses*, p 13.
20 Jonathan F.S. Post, *Henry Vaughan: The Unfolding Vision* (Princeton NJ: Princeton University Press, 1982), p. 178.

the Song of Solomon does little to dispel what he regards as the 'indeterminacy' of the poem's ending, since it puts off any arrival at a destination until external forces have completed their work: *'Arise O North, and come thou South-wind, and blow upon my garden, that the spices thereof may flow out'* (4:16).[21] Lewalski points out that this verse 'was glossed by Protestants as a reference to the soul's need for both the north winds of affliction and the refreshing south winds of God's grace' and so looks forward to 'the matter of the subsequent poems' in the first part of *Silex Scintillans*, which chart the poet's uneven 'progress toward sanctification'.[22]

Before he begins to negotiate the trials of his individual pilgrimage through the tract of time allotted to his generation, Vaughan undertakes a review of the universal features of human destiny: the stark physical reality of what it means to be mortal (in 'Death. A Dialogue'); redemption from death into eternal life (in 'Resurrection and Immortality'); and the ultimate fate that awaits every soul at the end of time (in 'Day of Judgement'). In order to invest his attempts to communicate these fundamental truths with authority, he tests them on touchstones mined from the Bible. A verse from the Old Testament confirms the Body's fear of its destination after death: *'A Land of darknesse, as darkenesse it selfe, and of the shadow of death, without any order, and where the light is as darknesse'* (Job 10:22). Before the second dialogue poem begins, a headnote from the New Testament endorses the Soul's assurance that Christ has prepared a *'new, and living way ... for us, through the veile, which is his flesh'* (Hebrews 10:20); and a postscript from one of the prophets confirms that Body and Soul will be reunited after a period of separation and looks forward to the subject of the third poem in the sequence: *'But goe thou thy way untill the end be, for thou shalt rest, and stand up in thy lot, at the end of the dayes'* (Daniel 12:13). Vaughan's dramatic evocation of that event is concluded beyond the text of the third poem with a warning about the need for readiness: *'Now the end of all things is at hand, be you therefore sober, and watching in prayer'* (1 Peter 4:7).[23] Post points out that this does not imply the kind of personal yearning for Christ's imminent return

---

21 John Wall, *Transformations of the Word: Spenser, Herbert, Vaughan* (Athens GA and London: University of Georgia Press, 1988), pp. 305–6, 310, 312–13. Vaughan cites this verse mistakenly as 'Cant. Cap. 5. Ver. 17' and substitutes Geneva's 'Arise' for AV's 'Awake', presumably to maintain the metaphor of an onward journey.

22 Lewalski, *Protestant Poetics*, p. 321.

23 See *HV Works*, pp. 59–64.

that provides a solution to the intractable problems of the present elsewhere in *Silex Scintillans*: 'historical time plays no part' in the structure of this poem, in which 'meditating on the End is a means for beginning the pilgrimage on the right foot'.[24]

Once the eternal context of human life has been rehearsed in these three poems, however, Vaughan does begin to address the burning issues of his own particular age and shows that they have already been distilled into words of Scripture more trustworthy than his own because uncontaminated by the partisanship of current controversy. In 'Religion', he first of all complains that the once clear spring of Religion has become a 'tainted sink' from which life-giving water no longer flows into the community of believers. Such a state of affairs was prefigured in an epigraph from the Song of Solomon, which had traditionally been interpreted as the marriage song of the Church with Christ: '*My sister, my spouse is as a garden Inclosed, as a Spring shut up, and a fountain sealed up*' (4:12).[25] Then, whereas 'Religion' expressed nostalgia for a time when there was still familiar 'Conf'rence' between heaven and earth in the narratives of the Old Testament, the speaker's 'roving Extasie / To find my Saviour' in the next poem, entitled 'The Search', takes him on a fruitless tour of New Testament sites associated with the life and death of Christ: Bethlehem, Egypt, the Temple in Jerusalem, Calvary, the tomb. Wall puts the failure of this quest down to the lack of an 'ongoing life of the church' that might give meaning to the historical narratives 'in the present'.[26] As the speaker is about to head for the 'Wilderness', where Christ faced the temptations of the devil and 'his bride' (that is, the Church) has now taken 'refuge', he hears a voice instructing him to 'Search well another world', advice which is amplified in a biblical postscript: '*That they should seeke the Lord, if happily they might feele after him, and find him, though he be not far off from every one of us, for in him we live, and move, and have our being*' (Acts 17: 27–8).[27] These authoritative words are from the sermon in which St Paul informs the inhabitants of Athens that God does not dwell 'in temples made with hands' but in the faithful followers who make up the Body of Christ in this world. The Apostle's words point the way forward for those dispossessed of the outward trappings of their religion: instead of seeking '*Manna*, where none is', they

---

24 Post, *The Unfolding Vision*, p. 193.
25 See *HV Works*, pp. 64–5.
26 Wall, *Transformations of the Word*, p. 322.
27 See 'The Search', *HV Works*, pp. 66–8.

should aim to keep their spiritual community intact by continuing to search within themselves for the Christ whose presence constitutes the true church. Without the epigraph and an awareness of its place in Paul's sermon, the full significance of the poet's account of his abortive quest in the poem would not be clear to prospective Anglican readers.

When it is read as the next item in this sequence of poems formally connected with specific biblical texts, 'Isaacs Marriage' takes on a meaning beyond the obvious contrast between Old Testament piety and contemporary licence, since the union of Isaac and Rebecca was traditionally regarded as a type of the marriage between Christ and the Church.[28] The poem that immediately follows it is the desperate cry for help by the 'ravish'd' and 'pillag'd' spouse of Christ in 'The Brittish Church', which is completed by a composite biblical epigraph in Latin, beginning: '*O Rosa Campi! O lilium Convallium!*' [O rose of the field! O lily of the valley!][29] Both exclamations are from the Song of Solomon (2:1), but the first is from the Latin translation by Tremellius, whose '*Rosa*' is presumably preferred to the Vulgate's '*flos*' [flower] because it had become symbolic of the Church of England during the troubles of the seventeenth century. In his poem 'Church-rents and schismes', for example, George Herbert had lamented that the 'health and beautie' of the once 'Brave rose' was being undermined from within by factional 'debates and fretting jealousies' and challenged from without by its Presbyterian 'neighbours' in the north.[30] The image was used by Vaughan himself in the autobiographical Latin poem, 'Ad Posteros', for an allegorical account of the triumph of the Puritans in the civil war:

> I lived at a time when religious schism had divided and fragmented the English people, amongst the furies of priest and populace. When these afflictions first raged through our pleasant land, a vile weed cast down the sacred rose, and the fountains were muddied; peace was drowned in the troubled waters, and a gloomy shadow overcast the days of splendour.[31]

---

28 See Alan Rudrum's 'Narrative, Typology and Politics in Henry Vaughan's "Isaac's Marriage"', *Scintilla*, 8 (2004), 10–11.

29 *HV Works*, pp. 71–2.

30 See *The English Poems of George Herbert*, ed. Helen Wilcox (Cambridge: Cambridge University Press, 2007), pp. 488–90. See also Wilcox's notes on ll. 1 and 22.

31 Translated from the Latin, *HV Works*, p. 164.

The rest of the epigraph to 'The Brittish Church' – *'quomodò nunc facta es pabulum Aprorum!'* [how are you now made food for swine!] – was taken from verse 13 of Psalm 80, which was headed by an explanatory note in early editions of the King James Bible: 'The Psalmist in his prayer complaineth of the miseries of the Church.'

After this comes 'The Lampe', which Post dismisses as 'a studious late night preparation for the End', working its way laboriously in the manner of an emblem poem towards the epigraph: *'Watch you therefore, for you know not when the master of the house commeth, at Even, or at mid-night, or at the Cock-crowing, or in the morning'* (Mark 13:35).[32] What needs to be taken into account, however, is the poem's connection with the parable of the ten virgins in St Matthew's gospel, who 'took their lamps, and went forth to meet the bridegroom'. Only the five who were wise enough to take 'oil in their vessels with their lamps' were able to respond when the cry came at midnight, 'Behold, the bridegroom cometh; go ye out to meet him'; and only they 'went in with him to the marriage: and the door was shut'. The parable ends with a verse that Vaughan's bible-using readers would have recognized as a parallel to the poem's epigraph from St Mark: 'Watch therefore, for ye know neither the day nor the hour wherein the Son of man cometh' (Matthew 25:1–13). The identification of 'the master of the house' with the 'bridegroom' forges a link with both the universal history and the more contemporary concerns about the Church explored in this opening group of poems . The verse in Mark, like the one in Matthew it brings to mind, is a call to all those who belong to the true spiritual community to be ready when Christ returns to welcome them into the wedding feast.

The final poem in this opening sequence, 'Man's fall, and Recovery', is a meditation by a generic 'Man' on his fall into sin in the person of Adam, his subsequent 'trespasses' against the laws written in the 'famous tables' brought down by Moses from Mount Sinai, and his redemption through the 'saving wound' of Christ. The story it tells and the doctrine it expounds are distilled in an appended verse from the Letter to the Romans: *'As by the offence of one, the fault came on all men to condemnation; So by the Righteousness of one, the benefit abounded towards all men to the Justification of life'* (5:18).[33] This is another instance of Vaughan selecting his bibli-

---

32 *HV Works*, pp. 72–3. For Post's comment, see *The Unfolding Vision*, p. 195.
33 *HV Works*, pp. 73–4. Vaughan wrongly places the quotation in Romans 18:19.

cal words carefully from the available versions. The moral contrast between Adam and Christ is sharpened by his adoption of 'the fault' from Geneva instead of the Authorised Version's *'judgment'* and the latter's 'righteousness' instead of Geneva's 'iustifying'; and doctrinal considerations may lie behind his preference for Geneva's 'the benefit abounded toward all men' over the *'the free gift came* upon all men' in the 1611 bible. Whatever the reasons for the eclectic origins of this epigraph, however, it provides an authoritative summary of the central issue of Sin and Salvation in the universal history of the human race to bring the introductory movement of *Silex Scintillans* to a fitting close.

IV

The next poem – coming after this sequence of nine supported by Scripture – is 'The Showre', which takes its inspiration from a natural phenomenon rather than the Bible. Of the sixty that follow it in the 1650 *Silex Scintillans*, only eight are accompanied by biblical texts, and these serve to enhance or complete the poem rather than primarily lending it external authority.[34] 'Midnight' is a nocturnal meditation on the influence of the stars, which Donald Dickson describes as 'one of Vaughan's most enigmatic poems'. Gazing at the sky, the speaker is struck by the contrast between the 'Emanations, / Quick vibrations / And bright stirs' of the astral bodies shining 'in their watches' and the 'thin Ejections, / Cold Affections, / And slow motions' of his own earth-bound breast. The conceit that the heavens are a 'firie-liquid light' that both '[s]treames, and flames' culminates in a plea for God to '[s]hine on this bloud, / And water in one beame' so that 'Both liquors' will 'burne, and streame' with a 'bright quicknes' and 'follow after / On that water, / Which thy spirit blowes!'[35] The significance of this imagery is not obvious, as Dickson notes, until the poem is 'read in the light of its guiding text', which makes it clear that its subject – never directly stated – is the poet's desire for the spiritual gifts that flow from baptism: '*I indeed baptize you with water unto repentance, but he that commeth after me, is mightier than I, whose shooes I am not worthy to beare, he shall baptize you with the holy Ghost, and with fire*' (Matthew 3:11).[36]

---

34 Among these eleven are 'And do they so?' and 'Buriall'.
35 *HV Works*, pp. 83–4.
36 For Dickson's analysis of this 'enigmatic' poem, see *The Fountain of Living Waters: The Typology of the Waters of Life in Herbert, Vaughan, and Traherne* (Columbia: University of Missouri Press, 1987), pp. 144–6.

The epigraph chosen for 'Disorder, and frailty' functions in a different way. After complaining at length about his repeated failure to maintain the eagerness with which he first responded to the life-giving presence of Christ, the poet prays at the end for his weak and perverse soul to be granted 'wings' and to be watered by 'grace'. An appended verse from one of the minor Prophets then alters the perspective from which the speaker has been surveying his lamentable history: 'O *Ephraim what shall I do unto thee? O Judah how shall I intreat thee? for thy goodness is as a morning Cloud, and as the early Dew it goeth away?*' (Hosea 6:4).[37] God's disappointment at the disorder and frailty of his creature is reinforced by the insertion of a word from the Geneva translation in place of the Authorised Version's repetition of the phrase, 'O Judah, *what shall I do unto thee?*' (italics added). There is a sharper sense of the Creator's yearning over his wayward people in Geneva's variation: 'O Judah, how shall I *entreat* thee?'[38] This radical shift from the self-absorbed complaint of the speaker to the cry of distress by a loving deity is one of Vaughan's most striking uses of an epigraph.

Towards the end of the 1650 *Silex Scintillans*, there is a cluster of four more poems tagged with biblical quotations. In 'The Pilgrimage', the epigraph from Hebrews 11:13 – '*And they Confessed, that they were strangers, and Pilgrims on the earth*' – generates an image of travelers in an alien land, forced to share Jacob's experience of lodging overnight in a nameless 'place', where they dream 'homes of their own' and pine like birds exiled from 'their native wood'. But the full implications of the final petition – 'So strengthen me, Lord, *all the way,* / That I may travel to thy Mount' (italics added) – are only realized when the wider context of the brief extract from Hebrews is brought into play. The '*strangers, and Pilgrims*' are, in fact, the long line of Old Testament patriarchs cited in Chapter 11 of the epistle as witnesses to the faith that sustained them, even though – as the earlier part of verse 13 recalls – their hopes were not fulfilled during their lifetimes:

> These all died in faith, not having received the promises, but having seen them afar off, and were persuaded of *them*, and embraced *them*, and confessed that they were strangers and pilgrims on the earth.

---

37 *HV Works*, pp. 108–10.
38 Ephraim and Judah were the two tribes of Israel occupying territory to the north and south of Jerusalem.

Once the reading experience is retrospectively informed by this context, the poem comes into focus as a message of encouragement to dispossessed Anglicans, who 'linger' like the poet as outcasts in their own land, to emulate their biblical predecessors and remain faithful in spite of 'tossings too and fro' and the prospect of enduring 'yet more days, more nights' of apparently fruitless 'travel' in this world.[39]

The epigraph to 'The Law, and the Gospel' – *'If ye love me, keep my Commandements'* (John 14:15) – is taken from the dialogue in which Christ prepares his disciples for his imminent death and resurrection and reiterates the 'new commandment' of love that supersedes the legalism of the moral code delivered to Moses on Mount Sinai: 'That ye love one another, as I have loved you' (John 13:34 and 15:12).[40] James Simmonds and Barbara Lewalski independently highlight the role of the epigraph of the third of these poems – 'The World' – in order to challenge a common misreading:

> *All that is in the world, the lust of the flesh, the lust of the Eys, and the pride of life, is not of the father, but is of the world.*
> *And the world passeth away, and the lusts thereof, but he that doth the will of God abideth for ever.*
> (First Epistle of St John 2:16–17)[41]

Both reject the view that 'The World' – with its famous opening line, 'I saw Eternity the other night' – is intended as 'a poem of mystical vision': the former argues that 'the whole composition is neither more nor less than an expansion and dramatization' of St John's words; the latter sees it as 'essentially a meditation' on the biblical text; and they agree that the figures of the lover, the statesman, and the miser should be seen as 'symbols of spiritual states' or as vividly realized 'emblems' derived from St John's three kinds of worldly temptations that distract human beings from the values of eternity.[42]

---

39 *HV Works*, pp. pp. 129–30.

40 *HV Works*, pp. 130–1. James Kuzner reads Vaughan's emphasis on the necessity for both love and fear in the context of the Reformation debate about grace and law and its expression in poems by Donne and Herbert. See 'Metaphysical Freedom', *Modern Language Quarterly*, 74 (2013), 470–6.

41 *HV Works*, pp. 131–3. The source of the epigraph is wrongly given as the Gospel of St John in the original edition.

42 James D. Simmonds, 'Vaughan's Masterpiece and Its Critics: "The World" Revaluated', *Studies in English Literature*, 2 (1962), 82, 89; Lewalski, *Protestant Poetics*, p. 344.

The fourth poem, 'The Mutinie', returns to the poet's personal pilgrimage through 'this vale / Of sin, and death' in search of a 'home' that lies beyond it. In the final stanza, he prays that he may not move the 'wrath' of 'the finisher / And Author of my faith' by disobeying his 'sacred and eternal wil', 'but soft and mild / Both live and die thy Child'.[43] At first sight, the epigraph that follows this conclusion seems enigmatic: *'To him that overcometh wil I give to eate of the hidden* Manna, *and I wil give him a white stone, and in the stone a new name written, which no man knoweth, saving he that receiveth it'* (Revelation 2:17). Once placed in its biblical and political contexts, however, its relevance to the poem begins to emerge. 'The Mutinie' records an occasion when the poet had 'murmur'd sore' against his Christian duty to be humble and patient in the face of defeat and oppression. But, as West has shown, Vaughan knew from his reading of the Revelation of St John that Christ's 'unique victory on the cross' had 'redefined for all time what it means to *overcome*'.[44] Vavasour Powell, one of Parliament's itinerant preachers, had taken a verse from St John's vision of the pronouncements made by the seven angels of the Apocalypse to the seven churches in Asia as the text for a Fast Sermon welcoming the Propagation Act of 1650 and justifying the Puritans' seizure of control in Wales: 'And he that overcometh, and keepeth my works vnto the end, to him will I give power over the nations: And he shall rule them with a rod of iron' (Revelation 2:26–7).[45] As the vision unfolds in the second and third chapters of Revelation, each of the seven churches in turn is warned against those among them 'which say they are apostles, and are not' (2:2) or 'which say they are Jews, and are not, but do lie' (3:9); and then commended for those among them who have had 'patience' and 'not fainted' (2:3) or have overcome 'tribulation' and been 'faithful unto death' (2:10). Whereas Powell had lighted upon the one prophecy (to the church in Thyatira) that used the word 'overcome' to vindicate the assumption of political power, Vaughan took his epigraph from the one (to the church in Pergamos) that most closely mirrored his own situation in the Usk valley: 'I know thy works, and where thou dwellest, *even* where Satan's seat *is*: and thou holdest fast my name, and hast not denied my faith' (2:13). The reference to 'Manna' in the verse attached to the poem as an

---

43 *HV Works*, pp. 133–4.
44 West, *Scripture Uses*, p. 226.
45 West quotes Powell's sermon from a volume entitled *Christ Exalted above All Creatures by God His Father*, published in 1651. See *Scripture Uses*, p. 217.

epigraph invokes the journey of the Israelites through the wilderness on their way to the promised land; and the obscure references to the 'white stone' and the 'new name' are explained in a marginal gloss in the Geneva bible, as rewards for the new kind of victory available to those who overcome in the manner redefined by the Cross:

> Suche a stone was wont to be giuen to them that had gotten anie victorie or prise, in signe of honour, and therefore it signifieth here a token of Gods fauour and grace: also it was a signe that one was cleared in iudgement. The newe name also signifieth, renome and honour.

Vaughan's epigraph from Revelation, therefore, both supplies a biblical vindication of his struggle to overcome a personal mutiny by softness and mildness, and extends – beyond the sequence of four scripturally grounded 'pilgrimage' poems that it brings to a close – to the even longer spiritual saga that begins with 'Regeneration' and is rounded off at the end of the 1650 volume with a biblical blessing and doxology from the General Epistle of Jude (vv. 24–5):

> *Now unto him that is able to keep us from falling, and to present us faultless before the presence of his glory with exceeding joy,*
> *To the only wise God, our Saviour, be glory, and majesty, Dominion and power, now and ever.* Amen.[46]

V

In general, the approach to biblical epigraphs in the new collection of poems added to *Silex Scintillans* in 1655 is different from that in the original collection of 1650. The earlier practice of printing out the words from the Bible is followed in only three instances. The first five stanzas of 'The Timber' contemplate the past and present experiences of a fallen tree, now wasting 'all senseless, cold and dark' upon a woodland floor, but stirring with a 'strange resentment' ('sense of grievance' or 'act of perceiving' *OED* n.1a, 3a) at the approach of a storm. In the sixth stanza, however, there is a transition, by way of a comparison with the post-death responses of a 'murthered man', to a meditation on sin, guilt and death that

---

46 These verses are printed at the end of the 1650 *Silex Scintillans*, set apart from the final poem, 'Begging', by a rule across the page. See *HV Works*, p. 146.

is capped by a verse from the New Testament: '*He that is dead, is freed from sin*' (Romans 6:7).[47] Pettet comments that these words 'furnished the primary and essential inspiration of the poem', in which the opening reverie about a natural phenomenon 'is merely introductory and illustrative'; the purpose of the epigraph is to show where 'the heart of the poem' lies.[48] Most of 'Jesus weeping (II)' expatiates on the simple detail from the story of the death of Lazarus – 'Jesus wept' (John 11:35) – cited as the poem's headnote. The final paragraph, however, expresses the poet's determination to devote himself to an answering grief, which will send him '(*Swan-like*) singing home'; and an appended verse from Psalm 73 – '*Whom have I in heaven but thee? and there is none upon earth, that I desire besides thee*' – provides an explanation of why he embraces the prospect of death with such paradoxical joy.[49] Similarly, a verse from St John's apocalyptic vision of heaven printed at the end of 'The Feast' – '*Blessed are they, which are called unto the marriage Supper of the Lamb!*' (Revelation 19:9) – is a fitting conclusion to a poem on the Eucharist that, as Noel Thomas observes, 'treats the Sacrament not so much as a means of sustaining man on earth but of giving him a foretaste of heaven'.[50] A further purpose may have been to remind readers of the ultimate union of Christ with the Church that had been dismantled and outlawed in contemporary Wales.

The other ten epigraphs in the second part of *Silex Scintillans* merely cite book, chapter, and verse beneath the title of the poem, in most cases to alert the reader to the scriptural source that has inspired what amounts to a 'spiritual exercise'.[51] In a few cases, however, the epigraph conditions the way in which the poem is read, although any explicit allusion to it is delayed until near the end. The speaker in 'The hidden Treasure', for example, searches for 'one grain of sincere light' amid the 'worlds lov'd wisdom' and the 'tainting appetites' that 'nature breeds', but finds that 'all is vanity'. Eventually, he determines to 'restore' to God all the gifts that have been bestowed upon him, 'But for one thing, though purchas'd once before'. And that 'one thing', for which he gladly gives up everything else, is identified in the verse from St Matthew's Gospel

---

47 *HV Works*, pp. 583–5.
48 Pettet, *Of Paradise and Light*, pp. 86–7.
49 *HV Works*, pp. 590–2.
50 Thomas, *Poet of Revelation*, p. 179. For 'The Feast', see *HV Works*, pp. 623–5.
51 Pettet suggests that these poems are inspired 'in a very literal sense' by the verse cited (*Of Paradise and Light*, p. 32).

cited at the head of the poem: 'Again, the kingdom of heaven is like unto treasure hid in a field; the which when a man hath found, he hideth, and for joy thereof goeth and selleth all that he hath, and buyeth that field' (13:44).[52]

Even the significance of the title of 'The Stone' does not begin to emerge until late in the text, when 'stones' are included among the 'dumb creatures' that cannot be bribed (like 'man') and or seduced (like 'woman') to conceal the 'dark designs' that the speaker wishes to keep hidden from God:

> Hence sand and dust
> Are shak'd for witnesses, and stones
> Which some think dead, shall all at once
> With one attesting voice detect
> Those secret sins we least suspect.

Vaughan then homes in on one particular stone that features in Joshua's recapitulation of the history of the Israelites from the times of Abraham and Moses to their settlement in the promised land, where some of them reverted to the worship of 'strange gods'. Joshua oversees a new covenant and sets up 'a great stone' beneath an oak tree 'by the Sanctuary of the Lord' (Joshua 24:1–26). All this leads up to the verse cited as the headnote of the poem: 'And Joshua said unto all the people, Behold, this stone shall be a witness unto us; for it hath heard all the words of the LORD which he spake unto us: it shall be therefore a witness unto you, lest ye deny your God' (Joshua 24:27). And it is this verse that supplies the necessary context for Vaughan's application of the story of the backsliding of the Jewish people to the contemporary sinner in his final paragraph:

> The *Law* delivered to the *Jews*,
> Who promis'd much, but did refuse
> Performance, will for that same deed
> Against them by a *stone* proceed.[53]

Wherever a source text is merely cited in a headnote, but especially in the last two examples, Vaughan must have expected his readers to be as familiar as he was with the Bible or at least to take the trouble to look up the

---

52 *HV Works*, pp. 608–9.
53 *HV Works*, pp. 602–4.

relevant verses as part of the experience of engaging with his poetry. This suggests that by the time he committed his new poems to print in 1655, he was both more confident in his public role – no longer feeling the need to spell out biblical authority for what he had to say – and also deliberately aiming at a 'fit audience' of like-minded 'scripture-users' among his contemporaries.

West Window (detail) Former Knights Hospitallers building adjacent to
St Basil's Church in Toller Fratrum, W Dorset
by David Brown

PAUL CONNOLLY

Mass

A sacral union. Forty-five thousand people
strangely yet easefully subdued and almost silent
save for the throb and pulse of the thing
a lilt of waves which dissipate but do not break
asway along to the putt of in-field balls,
cruelly attributed to the late Butch Wilkins
but so essential to these celebrants
and the tempo of their sacrifice,
the serene coda of a game long dead
time added on to no real purpose,
a rudimentary, expected home win
scarcely resented by the smiles
and amiable soft defiance of the away end.

The home goalie stretched, pranced on tiptoes
shimmied his trunk left and forward,
forward and right, then stretched and filled his vestments
with necessary expectation. Quiet gathered.

Then over the billowing nothingness
a trumpet pierced:
'Blow yer effin whistle referee yer soft get'
a reminder of what the rite required
approved in murmurs and laughter
for all was done now, missa est
chippies, telly and the boozer called
and some were leaving already.
A long ball went out for a goal kick.
A muffled but skull-voiced drone began.
A woman reached under her seat for a bag.
Blokes shifted their weight and puffed out,
more people left, a manager unfolded an arm
looked at his watch then refolded it.
The away goalie swept towards the ball
and drew a responsorial glissando from some of the crowd
who felt the next sounds before they came,
two short blasts then a longer trilling flourish,
a single voiced cheer spattering quickly away
into applause and final chants, into thought and
conversations.
Then with the always surprising speed and in a rumble
that ebbed towards the shock of stillness
everybody left

Spring Morning

Sun on drizzled grass was frosting,
day longed to achieve. Later,
the sky might jut and exhale, its breast
loom, its arms envelop the world,
but now swift lashes of wind
checked throngs of golden promise,
harried the tearing voice of crow flight,
and rippled the cowls on fat friar jackdaws.
A rabbit fled. Seeding, birth,
offers of flesh, ache and bread,
recall a receptionist's bruise-shut eye,
gallant tales of kneeling in puddles,
a sunbeam face, enamel and dentine
spumed in a basin, digits of love
kneading at guts, as anew and forever
the famous life-changing injuries
are proclaimed throughout the season of murder.

CHARLES WILKINSON

archaeologists in the air

archaeologists in the air
at evening deploy the sun's
low slant, so sorting glare
from shade, to rake the slope
for ramparts, the ribs
of decayed hill forts

roads asleep under grass,
nearby where villas dream
in deep avenues of earth,
still visible from the sky
as height lifts long-
buried lines from turf:
contours of marching
camps; tracings of dry
    streams restored

                  at daybreak
drench of light, a temple
is retrieved from a field:
image is form excavated
without trowel or trench

              & snow
on the mountain whitens
spurs & crests; the tracks
of drovers varnished, so
    delicate on ice

only the rites have vanished,
  the sounds slaughtered
    with the tribe, a last
      Ordivice, less than
        a plane's shadow
          now breaching
           speechless
            ground

Submarine off Wales

lost off the coast of Rhyl: *Resurgam*, its bow nuzzling the seabed; conning tower kinked inwards; iron sides stuccoed by anenomes, orange & white, the tentacles bent, testing quietly for cool currents. an increase in cloning kills competitors: no breath within but for the conger eel, timelessly resident: all this discovered after the scour:

& so to
bring back
the power
of buoyancy
as if it could ascend, the clergyman's dream,
upwards through pilot fish towards where water,
declining darkness, first greens in fluency before whitening
to the waves, past cloudy wrack-drift & above the shifting
glide & flick of translucent rays, to the surface, its play
glit & shimmer, the tower breaking in spray, the bow
slide-oiled & flashed with a new century's light

Note: *Resurgam* ('I shall rise again'). This name was given to a Victorian submarine that sank off the coast of Denbighshire in 1880.

hantant

        the return of rain after days of drought,
so damp renews soft residence on walls,
      & here's the present precipitate, tense
of enduring recurrence, watery revenants,
        their slippery walk, & each room as pure
attendance: a visitant past, the departed,
      now streaming, endure. A season of moist
spirits brings the longing for exorcism,
     the ghosts dispossessed & no coming back,
wet & contemporary to the hour. Spring
    should be a divestment of drenched
memory, a shedding in hope of summer's
    rest. Yet habitation is a drag of distance
within; each step going heavy with seconds
     of soaked inheritance: every home's a haunting

RIC HOOL

Sky Burial

Poetry has a hunger
              makes a fat person thin
turns thin to skeleton

Once you're in you're in   no way out
      this cage of lines

You ask
           Does it hurt?

What does is uncertainty

The first whisper of far-off wings

          those beaks
          come a-pecking

MARGARET WILMOT

New Year

How clear cut the mountains stand
against a flush of sky. And when a mist
slips low through the cleft, laps
at bales, slides its grey mantle over
the frozen bog – well, this is how
a new year arrives, leaving the old behind
in an invisible realm beyond sharp peaks.
The first of January…. Even the air feels new.
Cows at fodder in their barns, and me
ruminating too: relative to the years of my life
these weeks so few. Yet caught – casual flotsam? –
like flukes of an anchor wedged in rock.

Fritillaries

They come up in the clag beneath the holly,
where twigs collect, and not much grows
but docks. Was it here a boy once found the space
to hang a hammock and practice lolling?
I see his book, the conscious grin ...
The memory fades into the prickle
over these delicate bell-heads – back
after a dry summer, winter rain.

I buy seeds, fill compost trays,
water, try to think ahead – but find myself
kneeling to clear a collar around a clump
of fragile spears I'm sure I never planted.
It's what's here now which feels real.
Leaves poke from a stem I thought was dead.

ROGER GARFITT

The Good Son

in memory of Geoff Morris

There was a fathering care in his fingers that were never still.
As we talked at the roadside, he would be picking
the moss out of the window seals of my old Passat.
Or I'd see him out in the fields in his long coat,
spudding up docks so their leaves didn't rot in the hay.
Any gaps in the hedge he would plant with holly slips,
good medicine, he said, for the cattle, and I glimpsed
the lad the farmers' wives had chosen as their babysitter,
so often that the girl he was courting lost patience.
*If you don't marry them, somebody else comes by
and takes them – that's the worst of these women.*

Leaning back in his chair by the range, the kettle swung on a hook
over the open fire, he would look at me out of the afterlife
that was teatime, the knuckles on his left hand twisted
where he had caught them in the threshing machine hauled
from farm to farm during the War, making enough money
to lift his parents out of penury and buy Fos-y-Rhiew,
the Hollow in the Hill, fourteen acres he had turned
into a threadbare Eden, walking the cattle up
to graze along the grass verges once the Ridgeway
was tarmacked. *We're getting too thick on the patch
– that's the only thing.*

SAM GARVAN

Three Rivers

I have swum three rivers in this city
But they are all one
                              Schilling

        i.

Near dawn the Granta shivers,
though there is no breeze tonight
        along this portion of the river.

Each ripple catches on its tongue
the silver shilling of the moon.

A punt slides
        low in the water
            as if a bird alighting

                might sink the whole thing,

in it, only an old man drifting
    under the dark stone span of King's,
        a thousand moons appearing, swallowed up,
under Clare Bridge's golden parapets,
    her leafy scrolls,
        her seahorse necklaces.

Under the iron not-quite-there of Garrett Hostel Bridge
    the punt slides on
        low in the water

            as if a feather floating down

                might sink the whole thing.

ii.

Night-time already broached across the Cam.

The moment cattle grazing on the banks
        give up their outlines to the grass,

only their breathing left
        and their remembering.

iii.

The River of Sorrows
cuts an old course beneath these streets,

its rushing sound near Trinity
        mistaken once for a calamity of wings

            an angel conjured by mischance.

Under crook-legged Portugal Place
        it sends a chill that puts the *cavaquinhos* out of tune

and then through all our sad and sedentary layers
                it channels out

through greensand, mudstone,
under the meadowsilts of Lammas Land, and there

                a silent, upward leaching of
regret

into the grass

a little rill

a tiny creek fringed with foxtail

    with bittercress

        milkwort

and in the milkwort, all-seeing,
        an egret waits for everything to pass,
                white plumes black tipped,

the grass,
the milkwort's blue flowers,
the steam rising.

HOWARD WRIGHT

The Good Suit

My father argues himself into keeping the suit,
a fine woollen grey with charcoal pinstripe,

black silk lining and button-down inside pockets.
A good suit for a funeral. My mother says

it will probably be hers. Happily, he has never
had it on his back. Nevertheless, other mourners

hang around on the off-chance, old outfits
for special occasions. They stand in wardrobes

for years, worrying about death, the script
and empty stage, and the lack of rehearsal.

Everything

                                 The bedroom
gone thermo-nuclear. Coalsmoke in the rain.
A clinging childhood. The reek of rotten apples
where you turn the hedge,
                                 the spume
of mayflower across the fields. Two high
planes and a washed-out sun. The buntings
staying up until they fall down
                                 The beauty
in coincidence and a spill of stars; artistic
licence that never expires. Cheap music
that makes everything all right
                                 The lost note
in a peel of bells. The poetry of doubt.
Architecture and weather, some sleet
on the rooftops, cold in the bones.
                                 The silence
of work. The telephone pole, a junction
for wires slicing the sky into eight, nine,
like a pie-chart of Antarctica.
                                 The geometry
as icing on the cake. Coffee grounds
in the sink sluiced away but not before you see
in negative a quadrant of
                                 the universe.

Labor of Love
Richard Wilbur's
'A Plain Song for Comadre'

WILLIAM TATE

Nothing is unclean in itself; every part of the world and every calling in life is a revelation of the divine perfections, so that even the humblest day-laborer fulfils [sic] a divine calling. This is the democratic element in the doctrine of Calvin: there is with God no acceptance of persons; all men are equal before Him; even the humblest and meanest workman, if he be a believer, fills a place in the kingdom of God and stands as a colaborer with God in His presence. But—and this is the aristocratic, reverse side to the democratic view—every creature and every calling has its own peculiar nature: Church and state, the family and society, agriculture and commerce, art and science are all institutions and gifts of God, but each in itself is a special revelation of the divine will and therefore possesses its own nature. The unity and diversity in the whole world alike point back to the one sovereign, omnipotent, gracious and merciful will of God.[1]

The most frequently anthologized poem of the American poet Richard Wilbur, "Love Calls Us to the Things of This World," depicts the moment of disorientation experienced by a man awakened by the screech of pullies holding a laundry line. The man feels his awakening as his body's hijacking of his soul and at firsts resists, but the poem concludes with the soul "descend[ing]...in bitter love / To accept [his] waking body." That is to say, the man responds

---

[1] Herman Bavinck, "Calvin and Common Grace," *The Princeton Theological Review* (1909), 437–465, 464.

to the "call" specified in the title, accepting it as his *calling* to love the world. As the title indicates, the poem affirms the rightness of such love for all of "us," including us readers, yet this poem tells us next to nothing concerning what love for the things of the world will look like in practice. Wilbur returns to the question in another poem which appears eight poems later in the collection *Things of This World*. Like "Love Calls Us," the later poem, "A Plain Song for Comadre," brings together images of the morning sun, love, and a tantalizing glimpse of angels in order to characterize a life lived as an expression of love for God and others, a life which hears the divine call.

My argument will be that Wilbur, in "Plain Song," implicitly recognizes every legitimate human work performed for the love of God as a holy work, and it will be helpful to preview some of the implications of the claim with help from Nicholas Wolterstorff's *Reason within the Bounds of Religion*. Although Wolterstorff develops the point in light of particular Reformed emphases, Wilbur's poem indicates that much of what Wolterstorff formally describes might be tacitly endorsed by a Roman Catholic like Bruna Sandoval, the central character of Wilbur's poem.[2] As his title suggests, Wolterstorff focuses on the life of the mind, the vocation of scholars,[3] but he also places the academic calling within the bigger picture of Christian vocation more generally. Wolterstorff explains that thinkers who shared "the traditional Protestant view" "were struck by the 'dominion' passages [in Genesis 1 and 9]: subdue the earth and have dominion." (Wilbur directly alludes to these passages in "Mayflies," "Elsewhere," and "Lying.") Reformed thinkers, according to Wolterstorff,

> heard in these [verses] the message that humanity has a mandate from God—a "cultural mandate," as it came eventually to be called. Perhaps a plausible surface reading of the "dominion" words of the Old Testament is that [human beings are] there enjoined to engage

---

2 Wilbur's ecumenical style of Christianity combines characteristics which seem to me to derive from the Protestant New England cultural tradition which nurtured his poetry as well as from the more liturgical tradition of the Episcopal church where he worshipped as an adult. As my sources suggest, the focus on lay labor as a holy calling strikes me as more typical of Protestantism, though Wilbur considers it with reference to a Roman Catholic character.

3 Wolterstorff's focus derives in part from his response to Kant's *Religion within the Bounds of Reason Alone*, to which he alludes with his title.

in..."productive labor." But that is not the way the Protestant tradition characteristically understood them. It understood them as enjoining not only productive labor but the whole formation of culture. And it understood the development of scholarship as an essential component in cultural formation—not just as an instrument for self-improvement, and not just as an instrument for beneficial alteration of one's circumstances, but as something good in its own right. (140)

Wolterstorff goes on to fine-tune this Protestant view. As he explains, scholarship "constitutes only one" aspect of a full human response to the cultural mandate:

> And the Reformers saw no reason whatsoever for thinking it the noblest. Every occupation is to be a vocation before the face of God, each equal in nobility, if not in strategic importance, with the other. In God's sight learning is no more noble than farming, theorizing no more noble than cabinetmaking, scholarship than politics. All legitimate occupations have the same status before God of being obedient responses to the cultural mandate. (141)[4]

The most pertinent observation here with respect to Wilbur's poem is the reminder that we ought not to devalue professions which God approves. Wolterstorff has in mind theologians like Martin Luther and William Perkins, who both dignify common labor in their teaching. Wilbur might also have found a precedent in the seventeenth-century poet George Herbert, whose poem "The Elixir" identifies the "secret formula" (the idea suggested by the title) for making one's work holy. According to the fourth stanza of Herbert's poem, "A servant with this clause / Makes drudgerie divine / Who sweeps a room, as for thy laws, / Makes that and the action fine." That is, the servant of God, by applying the secret formula of

---

4 Wolterstorff's adjective, "legitimate," suggests one quick caveat: some occupations are *not* legitimate. When Prince Hal taunts the character Falstaff for his impenitent thievery in Shakespeare's *Henry IV, Part I*, Falstaff parodies the Protestant teaching in his response: "Why, Hal, 'tis my vocation, Hal. 'Tis no sin for a man to labour in his vocation." But Shakespeare, of course, means for us to recognize that Falstaff's defense is specious—some human activities don't count as vocations, as Wolterstorff remembers.

working for the love of God, makes mere labor a spiritual activity. Or appropriating Herbert's illustration by means of Wolterstorff's terms, the "legitimate occupation" of sweeping a room for God's sake has "status before God" as an "obedient response to the cultural mandate."

Martin Luther's point appears again in the thought of his modern namesake, Martin Luther King, Jr. King says, "If a man is called to be a street sweeper, he should sweep streets even as a Michelangelo painted, or Beethoven composed music or Shakespeare wrote poetry. He should sweep streets so well that all the hosts of heaven and earth will pause to say, 'Here lived a great street sweeper who did his job well.'"[5] Similarly, in his sermon "Learning in War-Time" (1939), C. S. Lewis says,

> The work of a Beethoven, and the work of a charwoman, become spiritual on precisely the same condition, that of being offered to God, of being done humbly "as to the Lord". This does not, of course, mean that it is for anyone a mere toss-up whether he should sweep rooms or compose symphonies. A mole must dig to the glory of God and a cock must crow.[6] We are members of one body, but differentiated members, each with his own vocation. A man's upbringing, his talents, his circumstances, are usually a tolerable index of his vocation.

Their shared insight is also the core of Wilbur's poem.

The central figure of this poem, the "comadre" of the title, is Bruna Sandoval. It is Bruna's job to clean the Roman Catholic mission church at San Ysidro,[7] and "plain song" in this context implies a commitment to the traditional liturgical forms of Roman Catholicism (and probably commitment to traditional practices more generally). At the same time, the phrase cooperates with other hints in the poem to indicate that Bruna is a no-nonsense, straightforward, plain and simple woman. "Comadre" usually denotes a "midwife," but may also imply one who is a gossip,

---

[5] I owe this reference to Hannah Tate Williams. King's text is available at http://www.goodreads.com/quotes/21045-if-a-man-is-called-to-be-a-street-sweeper.

[6] The particulars of this sentence remind me of details in Hopkins's sonnet "As kingfisher's catch fire" and in Wilbur's "Praise in Summer."

[7] Near Corrales, New Mexico. A few details of the history of the church appear at the website of the Corrales Historical Society, http://www.corraleshistory.com/html/the_old_church.html.

perhaps perceived by her neighbors as a busybody. Several details of the poem imply that this particular comadre is prim and stern in her demeanor, maybe even a little self-righteous. Nevertheless, the poem commends her very human mode of loving. In complementary contrast with the speculative thinker in "Love Calls Us," Bruna is sensibly down-to-earth.

Bruna is not actually named until the fifth stanza, where the poem turns to focus on the particulars of her service to the parish. Before the end of the fourth stanza, the poem's observations, developed within and in response to three questions, appear generic, yet the questions may plausibly be understood as parts of the internal conversation which Bruna has had with herself while doing her work over many years. The language may be more sophisticated than Bruna would use in her own speech, but the tone and perceptions revealed by the questions are hers. The first question admits that verifiable proofs of spiritual realities aren't always available, but considers this state of affairs reasonable. According to lines one through five, "Though the unseen may vanish, though insight fails / And doubter and downcast saint / Join in the same complaint, / What holy things were ever frightened off / By a fly's buzz, or itches, or a cough?" Bruna recognizes and accepts that, in the experience of normal Christian life, visible confirmation of spiritual realities is likely to be rare. The apparent redundancy of "the unseen...vanish[ing]" underscores the rarity of visions. Potentially more troubling for the plain believer, the internal vision of "insight," seeing with the heart, also "fails," so that the emotional experience of the discouraged and "downcast saint," who longs for confirmation of her faith, may seem indistinguishable from the emotional experience of the "doubter," the unbelieving skeptic. Though for different reasons, both profoundly feel the lack of visible or tangible confirmation of the truth that God is, and that He is at work in the world. Within the question, however, these details are governed by the concessive "though," and Bruna responds with mild scorn: "What holy things were ever frightened off" by trivial inconveniences like flies buzzing?[8] Having asked (or felt) her first question, Bruna responds

---

8 My colleague Gwen Macallister has suggested an allusion to Emily Dickinson's "I Heard a Fly Buzz." The suggestion is quite plausible, given Wilbur's appreciation of Dickinson (see his essay "Sumptuous Destitution" in *The Catbird's Song*). The first poem in the collection *Things of This World* is "Altitudes." The poem is organized in two parts; the first section defines the heaven-implying, angel-inhabited space of a cathedral dome, while the second defines the creative space of the cupola in Dickinson's father's house. The space is situated above "the dark house below, so full

with staunch affirmation. Holy things are "Harder than nails," according to lines six and seven. The conventional comparison indicates that holy things are somehow more fully real than merely material things; at the same time, the phrase reveals something of the toughness of Bruna's character; hers is a hard spirituality.

She goes on to affirm, in lines seven through ten, that holy things are "more warmly constant than the sun, / At whose continual sign / The dimly prompted vine / Upbraids itself to a green excellence." We should pause to appreciate that "upbraids" is a wonderful pun. As we normally use it, this word means "rebukes," and in this meaning reveals Bruna's characteristic strictness. In context, however, Wilbur also achieves the etymologically suggested rightness of using the word to describe the intertwining of the vine's tendrils as it grows sunward.[9] These lines also echo "Love Calls Us," in which "the sun acknowledges / With a warm look the world's hunks and colors," so that the sun's condescension in enlivening the world's matter figures the soul's condescension to inhabit the body. Similarly in "Plain Song" the sun shines on the earthly and material vine, prompting its growth. The image implies that the influence of the invisible and spiritual "holy things" commonly appears, not in astonishing displays, but in subtle, possibly ambiguous, effects.[10] As Jesus tells Nicodemus in John 3, the wind blows wherever it wants, and we're aware of the wind because we see its effects, not because we can see the wind itself. The work of the spirit, like the work

---

of eyes / In mirrors and of shut-in flies" (22–23). "Altitudes" is followed by "Love Calls Us" (the second poem in the collection) and "Plain Song" (the ninth poem). Someone reading through the collection will be reminded of Dickinson's fly by the first poem and is likely to think of it again in reading "Plain Song." In the manner of a diptych, "Altitudes" identifies contrasts, but also suggests analogies between the sacred space of the cathedral dome and the sacred elevation of Dickinson's privacy. Anticipating the richly ambiguous depiction of angels in "Love Calls Us," "Altitudes" refers to "the race / Whom we imagine...wholly at home" (3–4) within the splendor of the dome, "conversing in that precious light" where "They chat no doubt of love" (8–9). In a contrasting parallel, Dickinson inhabits "the little cupola" (20) of her "father's house" (18) which is "furnished only with the sun" (24; compare the sun in both "Love Calls Us" and "Plain Song").

9 In conversation Maggie Luke suggested to me the possibility of an allusion to the first part of John 15, where Jesus says "I am the vine" and discusses what love looks like; she also noticed an intriguing resonance with "braids down" in the first stanza of "A Baroque Wall-Fountain in the Villa Sciarra."

10 Paul's consideration of the invisible things of God in Romans 1:18ff. is probably relevant.

of the wind and the sun, may be subtle, so that the influence isn't immediately obvious.

In lines eleven through fourteen the image of the constant sun, dependable in its daily rising, broadens into an awareness of the daily cycle of day and night with a new question: "What evening, when the slow and forced expense / Of sweat is done, / Does not the dark come flooding the straight furrow / Or filling the well-made bowl?" The "forced expense of sweat" fulfills the primal curse of burdensome daily labor. God tells Adam, in Genesis 3:17–19, "cursed is the ground because of you; in pain you shall eat of it all the days of your life; thorns and thistles it shall bring forth for you; and you shall eat the plants of the field. By the sweat of your face you shall eat bread, till you return to the ground." The darkness which floods the straight furrow and fills the well-made bowl, thus obscuring the works of human hands, brings with it a nightly reminder that the curse remains in effect. By using the participle "flooding," Wilbur prompts our awareness of another judgment on human sin which follows hard on the heels of the curse, the great flood which only those taken into the ark survived.

Even before their sin, however, Adam and Eve were charged with understanding and cultivating the earth,[11] as Wolterstorff has reminded us, and that original responsibility, though made burdensome by the curse, remains the responsibility of human beings. After the Genesis flood, the original cultural calling is renewed for Adam and Eve's descendants in God's covenant with Noah.[12] So the products of human cultural activity named in Wilbur's poem, the furrow, the bowl, and the chimney mentioned a few lines farther on, *matter* in spite of the curse. This is already implied by the description of the furrow as "straight," indicating that the plow has been guided by a farmer who, to recall Jesus' language in Luke 9:62, having set his hand to the plow, has not looked aside, but has guided the plow faithfully. Similarly, the bowl is well-made, the work of a careful potter. (Jeremiah 18:4 is suggestive here.) Developing the implications, the third question of the poem, in lines fifteen through seventeen, raises the possibility that human cultural labor resists the darkness: "What night will not the whole / Sky with its clear studs," the stars, "and steady spheres / Turn on a sound chimney?" The idea here is that, by providing a focus which establishes a point

---

[11] See Genesis 1:28–31. Notice that the alternation of morning and evening in the creation account establishes the pattern for the same alternation in the poem.

[12] See Genesis 9:1–7.

of view, human cultural work (the well-built chimney) gives shape to the world, including even the darkness.[13] Figuratively, the work of human hands "takes dominion." The soundness of the chimney provides a point of reference for human observation of the turning of the spheres, the apparent movement of the stars across the night sky, and the movement of the spheres anticipates and promises the daily return of the sun.

The alternation of night and day, sunset and sunrise, recalls (to my mind) Gerard Manley Hopkins' use of the same imagery in the sonnet "God's Grandeur." After affirming that God's grandeur is gloriously manifest throughout the creation, the sonnet asks why human beings fail to see God's glory and answers that they have been desensitized by labor as it has been conditioned by the fall and made burdensome by the curse: "all is seared with trade; bleared, smeared with toil" (6). Yet in spite of sin, God continues to work, renewing the broken creation[14] in the *re*-creative power of the resurrection. For Hopkins, as for Wilbur, the darkness of the night pictures the evil conditions resulting from the fall, but every morning pictures and promises ultimate renewal, so that "though the last lights off the black West went / Oh, morning, at the brown brink eastward springs— / Because the Holy Ghost over the bent / World broods with warm breast and with ah! bright wings." This is that same Spirit whose re-creative work is as evident—and as hidden—as the work of the wind in Jesus' description of that work to Nicodemus, and the re-creation is the new birth which Jesus thereby offers to Nicodemus.

The image of the nightly turning of the spheres marks the turning point of "A Plain Song for Comadre," since it's here in the poem that Bruna Sandoval comes into focus. Setting aside abstraction and figure, the poem states directly that "It is seventeen years / Come tomorrow / That Bruna Sandoval has kept the church / Of San Ysidro" (17–20). The turn seems abrupt until we realize that Bruna's labor also, in some way like the sunrise, challenges the darkness. The casual and conventional way we hear the phrase "come tomorrow" deepens in our awareness that this particular tomorrow is the

---

13 In its effect the chimney thus resembles the jar (probably, significantly, a "Dominion" brand canning jar) which domesticates the wilderness around it in Wallace Stevens's "Anecdote of the Jar." I'm suggesting that the "secondary creation" of the poet (and even human activity more generally) has the potential both to echo God's primary creation and to participate in, and somehow contribute to, God's re-creative activity in the redemption of the world.

14 See Romans 8:18–25.

culmination of seventeen years of tomorrows in which the constant sun has returned with morning, pushing aside the darkness of the night, and in which Bruna has faithfully done her work, resisting the curse. Her daily labor includes, according to lines twenty through twenty-two, "sweeping / And scrubbing the aisles, keeping / The candlesticks and plaster faces bright" (20–22). The "dust and sin"[15] of the world contaminate even the sanctuary—the place of holy things—and even the human artifacts dedicated for use in worship and intended as material representations of holy things, the candlesticks and images that feature in Bruna's devotion. With a constancy as reliable as that of the sun, which God made "to separate the day from the night" and "to rule the day" in steadfast predictability,[16] Bruna keeps order in the church of San Ysidro. The sun in its sphere and Bruna in hers each performs the task which God has appointed.

What is it that motivates Bruna Sandoval? In one sense she is pointedly like the "doubter and downcast saint" mentioned in line two, for whom the unseen has vanished. In all the seventeen years of her work in the church, Bruna has been like them in that she has "seen no visions," according to line twenty-three. She doesn't expect to become another Julian of Norwich or Teresa of Avila. Instead, her ordinary, down-to-earth visions are visions of "the thing done right." She sees the work that needs to be done and knows how to do it, "From the clay porch" at the entrance of the church, all the way "To the white altar" at the front (24–25). So what motivates Bruna Sandoval? What distinguishes her from the "downcast saint" (or helps her get beyond being downcast, if that is part of her experience)? The poem answers in a single word: *love*. "For love and in all weathers / This is what she has done" according to lines twenty-five and twenty-six.[17] By passing quickly from the one word to the recognition that she has done her work "in all weathers," the poem

---

15 I borrow the phrase from George Herbert's "Love (III)."
16 See Genesis 1:14–19.
17 One of the characters in George Eliot's *Middlemarch* describes another character in a way that brings out implications of Wilbur's presentation of Bruna Sandoval:
Her full nature...spent itself in channels which had no great name on the earth. But the effect of her *being* on those around her was incalculably diffusive: for the growing good of the world is partly dependent on unhistoric acts [that is, acts not included in history books, acts that don't make history]; and [the fact] that things are not so ill with you and me as they might have been is half-owing to the number who lived faithfully a hidden life, and rest in unvisited tombs.
Cited by Steven Garber in *Visions of Vocation: Common Grace for the Common Good* (Downers Grove, IL: InterVarsity Press, 2004), 88.

makes it clear that Bruna doesn't linger over love regarded as a feeling. She isn't one to talk much about how she feels. She is rather one whose principle vision is simply seeing what needs to be done and whose primary expression of love is in her doing of what needs to be done, regardless of the weather. In the book *Visions of Vocation* Steven Garber describes a successful life as "long obedience in the same direction." Long obedience in the same direction—the straight furrow, the seventeen years of reliability—exactly expresses the way Bruna puts into practice her love for God.

And yet. Though Bruna expects no ecstatic vision, and experiences none, the final lines of the poem suggest that even in her daily work, there is adequate vision for one with eyes to see; if not exactly a vision, there is a glimpse for her of spiritual realities, even in her work. Moreover, for those who have the eyes to recognize it in her work, there is *precisely in her faithfulness* a glimpse of those same realities. These final lines, twenty-seven through thirty, again invoke the morning: "Sometimes the early sun / Shines as she flings the scrubwater out, with a crash / Of grimy rainbows,[18] and the stained suds flash / Like angel-feathers." The same sun that shines on the vine as a sign of invisible things back in the second stanza, the same sun that "acknowledges / With a warm look the world's hunks and colors" in "Love Calls Us to the Things of This World," draws color from Bruna's dirty scrubwater.[19] By means of this divine refraction, Bruna's faithful dedication to the daily work of renewal shines in the sight of heaven, making space for glimpses of angels, not in spite of, but precisely *in* the daily effort.

---

18 After "flooding" in line 13, "rainbows" suggests the divine promise to Noah that God will not again destroy the earth by flood (see Genesis 9:1–17). (There is here a possible connection with "Still, Citizen Sparrow.") The image also reminds me of "the pool of bilge / where oil had spread a rainbow" so that "everything was rainbow, rainbow, rainbow!" in Elizabeth Bishop's "The Fish" (78–9 and 85), included in *Poems* (New York: Farrar, Strauss and Giroux, 2011).

19 The freshly washed laundry in "Love Calls Us" is the mundane work of hands reddened by the heat of hot water, and that same laundry "dances...in the sight of heaven" (20) as if it had been inspired by angels—even though the clothing will be dirtied again in the daily use of thieves and lovers and even nuns. Bruna's likeness with the nuns of "Love Calls Us" is made especially apparent in a passage from a commencement address by Wilbur. In "A Speech at a Ceremony" Wilbur comments that "even monks and nuns, who have a special professional concern with last things, pass toward them by way of each day's duties, each day's canonical hours, and the feasts of the church year" (*Responses* [New York: Harcourt Brace Jovanovich, 1976], 71).

Llanrhychwyn Church of St Rhychwyn, Llanrhychwyn, in remote farmland above the Conwy valley north of Bettws-y-Coed. Possibly founded by Llywelyn the Great in c 1200
by David Brown

MICHAEL HENRY

The Authority Of Death

Your old Corsa stalled halfway up Aggs Hill.
"It's the steepest bit," you said. "We'll back down."
The sun caught your prophet-white hair and beard.
Eighty-seven years old, acting twenty.

You offered a metaphorical lifebelt of trust
and I took my place in the passenger's seat,
expecting to meet a tractor or a dustcart
as you reversed in neutral down the hill.

"It's flatter here," you said, backing into the bank.
At the fifth attempt the engine caught
and with a *pétarade* of hiccupping
and tittupping we were up and away.

Jump-cut to your hospital bed where
I offer you my arm as a lifeline
and feel the warmth of your stalling strength.
"We must go backwards to go forwards," I say.

I wish time didn't register on your life-dial
as I back into the labyrinthine corridors,
pop into the chapel to collect points of light
for your reverend-white hair, then out into

the chalky September sky where day cedes to
the authority of night and life to the authority
of death, where superannuated leaves hang
onto twigs and one old man is livid not to live.

HELEN OVERELL

Mending

Amidst the chaos, infold of scar-shine —
within of sea shell, without of hazel nut,

the puckered curve a constant reminder —
new growth that shields old hurt, the in-built healing

renewed throughout the years as though a pearl
shone there, glimmer of hope making whole the hours,

the hold-fast days splashed and splattered with light
that sifts the shadows, lifts the stumbling heart.

Three Yellow Butterflies

We sit in the garden this May month drenched in light –
drifts of sage, cranesbill, cascades of wild roses loud with bees,

leaf-green shade leavened with blue snippets of periwinkle,
scatterings of alkanet, alizarin glow of many-petalled peonies,

here, mid-air, in ribboned flight, three yellow butterflies –
old souls making way for those as yet unfurled, still in bud –

dance wing-tip close – notes on a stave, chord, arpeggio –
weaving song throughout sky-enfolded world.

JOCK STEIN

Exodus

Psalm 114
'Dante's angel is at the helm of a boat in which more than a
hundred spirits are singing Psalm 114'   Edward Clarke

    Dante came to meet me, walking on his hands
    – and knees – hound hermeneut with four tails,
    nose to a trail he feels and understands.

    Each tail wagged the dog to the altar rails:
    Judah became temple, Israel God's dwelling
    place, layers of meaning driven nails

    into the story board of earth, spelling
    out God's saving purpose, sowing seeds
    of greater morning glory, show-and-telling

    Bible meanings in these crazy deeds.
    Mountains go mad with magma melt,
    cliffs are cleft with cataracts, God reads

    his play on the stage of Sinai, his belt
    tight round his tribe, only let out a notch
    when Moses intercedes with heart-felt

    cries for those who cannot stay on watch
    while God gives Moses temple time.
    Dante finds his feet, plays hopscotch

    with his Classic friend, stirring the lime
    between the polysemous squares
    of old interpretation, adding rhyme

    to link the Exodus to all of us. He bares
    his chest: it's gospel truth, he swears.

EVE JACKSON

When the World Was Quiet

A distant thrum; a generator, an engine, something
that forgot to stop or be stopped as I watch
birds embolden across the margin

of their usual edgy presence; pen themselves:
sparrow, wren, finch; that one blackbird
scatting in jazzy colour all his wants and wishes

across my morning. Bird-space refills
wing by wing, each flap counted; a measure
of how far they have come; can go.

Below, a dunnock picks up secrets in full view
of the window. A pigeon hunkers on the fence;
sunset swell of each steady breath.

Bedstraw and ox-eye daisies yawn
across tarmac. Buttercups, not under
the chin, but enough yellow to seep beneath skin.

Splashes of white-light on leaves trickle
from trees, fall on these overgrown paths. I wade
waist high through the quiet of an afternoon.

Beyond a Dream

A boy is climbing a tree,
his hands, arms, legs believe;
his head leads the way

The tree is not there yet, but one day
a boy will find a seed, swaddle it
against shrivel and snap of sapling

A boy is a caterpillar; stretch and pull
of green jumper up the trunk. In the canopy
he droops, legs dangle like pliable willow

The tree that is not there yet *knows*
limbs crack, roots network to nowhere,
leaves cackle downwards in stingy fists

A boy is balanced beneath a senseless sky, where
nothing catches the eye, ears sting with stillness
and a violent sun threatens to suck him in

The tree that is not there yet will one day
be nurtured into *treeness*, grow beyond a dream
through seasons – as the boy imagines them to be

MATTHEW STEWART

In the Middle

Caught in my forties between plaintive calls
from my mother and a Playstation 4
that leaves my son deaf to any advice,
today, at least, I sit and watch them chat
at this excuse for a celebration.

Over pudding, she demands I translate
his latest spurt from his centimetres
to her inches before I translate back
her perfect guess of just how close he is
to overtaking me.

JONATHAN WOODING

The Book of Jashar

*And there was no day like that before it or after it, that the
LORD hearkened unto the voice of a man*
                    The Book of Joshua, 10:14

*A book based on one of the slovenly ... abridgements of the
Pentateuch ... by some ignorant Monk*
          Samuel Taylor Coleridge, Collected Letters

I.
Stop this. The roots outrun the book.
A book's not wanted. Not *The Book of Jashar*.
The book's been taken out. Jashar is sanguine.

Nothing looks back at Jashar, out of time.
Blackberries still apparent (in parenthesis),
and buddleia breezy and idling with bees.

The weather's not pretence. It doesn't mind
Jashar's millenarian prize – *all
covetousness and ambition satisfied.*

Jashar's into ruddy leaves, blood-drop apples,
and the final flights of tortoiseshell butterflies,
unmemoried, immemorial

as the pitched orison and bitter crux
of a solitary, querulous buzzard's cry,
counting her bestial store.

Disordinate words don't do indifference.
At the gates here are bronze peony leaves,
high breezes preening the silver birch,

and – what do I know? – a jet-spangled fly
cursive and importunate as handwriting
in a bloodshot, wine-dark book.

II.
I swear the small birds are interested
in what I am doing. Should they want
to be in *The Book*, maybe. *Pilpul, pilpul.*

A chaffinch, comfortable as a cat,
decorates the naked apple tree.
Four peeky sparrows are showing off

on the lichened roof of the broken summerhouse.
Then they take high places
in a humiliated sapling. I swear they're interested.

The morning air is baffled, shot through
with the planetary; planetary mist – you know.
As if my milky eye were outside.

The eye fails to deride her circumstance.
All is self-derision; air's all
up in the air, internally murky. *Pilpul.*

The small birds won't leave the trees alone.
Poetry becomes a thing of the past.
Mind, let's say, unbaffled,

exact in the outside, its blink, its *pilpul*, yes.
The small birds are interested.
Ricercar, ricercar, ricercar.

You can't believe it. So, let me say
it's a page from the Talmud, yay, from the Zohar.
All these small birds. This milky stuff

in the garden air, this proleptic dew
all over grass blades and skeletal tree life.
Pilpul. Pilpul. Mind, I tell you.

TOM GOUTHWAITE

Quiet Space

If there was sorrow
in this fallen reed,
I cannot know its voice

or guess the whispers
of its vanished song
above a water-light
of broken cloud,

or if its shadow
with a hundred thousand others
made a fleeting quorum
for their requiem,

or if these others,
cut and bundled now,
will ever touch the air
with sound again;

but this quiet space,
this empty marsh-light
over shining water,
was their fellow pilgrim.

LESLEY SAUNDERS

Croquembouche

A mountain of free-standing choux pastry stuffed with cream, held together by chocolate and caramel, then bejewelled with sugared almonds and crystallised roses and dusted with icing sugar…

It was Michel Roux holding his frail artifice aloft
in a Paris street *en route* from the *maître-pâtissier*
to his home for a family party that had me
dissolved in tears of disbelief and joy, enfolded
in contemplation of the divine in material form –
such gravity-defying confection, such rich food
for the eyes of the soul, and so preposterously
more than enough to remind us that one day
we too will be as uplifted in rapture as a sugar-rose,
spun finer than a thread of shining caramel,
our sweet flesh will be as candied apricots,
exquisite riposte to catastrophe and apocalypse
and the great night that lies at our feet; incarnated
with all compassion, then broken and consumed.

Placebo

Some people even asked, 'Where can I get some of those placebos I saw on TV?' –
    Dr Jeremy Howick, Oxford University Centre
        for Evidence-Based Medicine

Am I so hard to please? It's said red pills
work less efficiently than blue or yellow ones
(though Latin can be a panacea in itself),
the side-effects of self-deception hidden
in the small print on the maker's leaflet
folded into a wad inside the packet –
better to self-medicate with a boxed set
of afternoon crime dramas where shoulders
are prosthetised with satin pads and blood's
shed recklessly as claret on Turkish rugs:
libations to the jealous watchful gods,
the things done and left undone that upbraid me
in the night, their abrasions and wistful pains
as of a missing limb. In the grey hour of morning
or was it far into evening a glimmer of insight
pale as aspirin hovered in the pathless orchard
of my mind like a salvific, and finally I realised
there's no pleasing to be had, no clemency
for *tristitia*. I sit here in my elegant skin, implacable.

Holiness From Abroad: George Herbert's Dialogue with St. François and Henry Vaughan's Emulation of St. Paulinus

JONATHAN NAUMAN

Ever since Louis Martz ventured to observe a Salesian accent and attitude in *The Temple*, highlighting for comparison St. François's devotional pursuit of internal experience of God's presence, the "ease and familiarity" of his "imagery from everyday life," his simplicity in style and use of witty conceits "bellement et doucement,"[1] there has been some critical exchange over the nature and extent of the English poet's awareness of *An Introduction to the Devout Life*.[2] Careful attention to Herbert's friendship with Nicholas Ferrar and to the poet's involvement with "the translation and publication of European texts" at Little Gidding[3] leaves small doubt that George Herbert had some interest in St. François's work and some

---

1 Louis L. Martz, *The Poetry of Meditation*, rev. ed. (New Haven and London: Yale University Press, 1962), pp. 250, 253, 259.

2 Barbara Lewalski offers, in *Protestant Poetics and the Seventeenth Century Religious Lyric* (Princeton, NJ: Princeton University Press, 1979), p. 283, "biblical genre theory, biblical tropes, Protestant ways with emblem, metaphor, and typology, and Protestant theory regarding the uses of art in religious subjects" as "a necessary corrective" to Martz's recourse to continental Roman Catholic devotional works such as St. François's *Introduction*. Ensuing studies have alluded to St. François in lists of Roman Catholic texts that have been compared with Herbert's; see, for example, Gene Edward Veith, Jr., *Reformation Spirituality: The Religion of George Herbert* (Lewisburg, PA: Bucknell University Press, 1985), p. 57, and Stanley Stewart, *George Herbert* (Boston, MA: Twayne, 1986), p. 58. Elizabeth Clarke re-examines Martz's comparisons between St. François and Herbert in detail in her chapter on *"An Introduction to the Devout Life* and *The Temple*: 'The Poetry of Meditation' or 'Private Ejaculations'?" in *Theory and Theology in George Herbert's Poetry* (Oxford: Clarendon Press, 1997), pp. 71–126.

3 Clarke, pp. 72–73.

acquaintance with it; and even apart from the Ferrars, it must be said that the *Introduction* was in Herbert's time a cultural phenomenon that would not easily be ignored by an Englishman with international or even merely domestic knowledge of current movements in Christian devotion. The French bishop's book had gained immediate popular following after its first publication in 1609, and by the time George Herbert was ordained deacon it had been translated into Italian, English, Flemish, Latin, and Spanish.[4] As Elizabeth Clarke has pointed out,[5] the *Introduction* was probably not one of the books included in a shipment from France mentioned in one of Herbert's early letters, for the poet described the volumes in that shipment as "not to be got in England."[6] Even if this letter of Herbert's was written at the earliest of possible dates proposed by Amy Charles,[7] it would still be preceded by three editions of the first English translation of St. François's manual.

---

4 St. Francis de Sales, *Introduction to the Devout Life*, tr. John K. Ryan (New York: Image, 2014), pp. 9–10. See also John Yakesley's dedication of his pioneering translation of *An Introduction to a Devoute Life* (Douai: G. Patté for J. Heigham, 1613) "To the right virtuous gentlewoman Mistris Anne Roper, daughter to the right worshipfull Sir William Roper, of Well-Hall in Eltham": "This excellent summarie of spirituall life (*Right worshipfull and trulie Religious*) hath gained so great credit with all devout minds, for the exceeding profit and delight which they have found by perusing it: that no booke whatsoever hath been in so short a time, so often, and in so manie places reprinted; none by so manie men, and those of so great judgement, and in such varietie of bookes treating of the same subject, so much commended. Litle indeed it is in quantitie, but in substance, and in effect, (as I may say) infinite. Like the philosophers stone, which being but small in bignes, and not verie beautifull in shew, conteineth in it the seedes of all metalls, & with the onely touch, changeth baser metalls into the soveraignest of all, which is gold, the sole governour now, of this iron world. For even so truly not onely in my judgement, (which in these heavenly matters reacheth but low) but in the judgement of great divines, and very holy men, there hath not come out any abridgement of devotion like this, conteining so copiouslie in few leaves, so plainlie in sweet language, so profitablie and aptlie for practize of all men, the rules and instruction of spirituall perfection, nor so pregnant in efficacie, to convert the iron affections of our soules, into the golden virtue of charitie, and true devotion the queene of virtues, that enamoureth God him self with her heavenlie beautie" (pp. A2^r-A3^r). Quotations below from this translation of de Sales's work will be cited by signature, as pagination is not consistent. (Exemplar consulted: Bodleian Vet. E2 g.8.)

5 Clarke, p. 72.

6 F. E. Hutchinson, ed., *The Works of George Herbert* (Oxford: Clarendon Press, 1941), pp. 366–367. Citations from Herbert's works below are from this edition.

7 Hutchinson dates this letter in 1618 because Herbert says the books have been shipped by his brother Henry, who is known to have been in Paris during that year (p. 579). Amy Charles, however, states that 1618 is "probably too late," and

But if there is every reason to believe that George Herbert was familiar with and interested in the *Introduction*, there is also more than sufficient evidence to assume that the poet would regard François de Sales, Roman Catholic Bishop of Geneva, from a measured patriotic distance, and his *Introduction* as an implicit challenge, the work of a worthy opponent. When Herbert urged Nicholas Ferrar to publish Valdesso's *Considerations*, his first reason for doing so was "that God in the midst of Popery should open the eyes of one to understand and express so clearly and excellently the intent of the Gospell in the acceptation of Christs righteousnesse ... a thing strangely buried, and darkned by the Adversaries, and their great stumbling-block" (304–305). The Bishop of Geneva was not like Valdesso a Roman Catholic inclined toward Reformed theology, but a famous exponent of the Roman communion known for his efforts toward reconversion of Calvinists to Catholicism in the Chablais. In short, it is no surprise that George Herbert the Anglican Protestant, however knowledgeable of the *Introduction*, should have left no clear reference to the work or explicit mention of its writer.

But one must remember in this context that Theodore Beza himself, in his old age, had granted the young François de Sales an audience, irenically debating some doctrinal tenets with him, the two men treating each other with sincerity and courtesy before parting unconverted, each still convinced of his own particular Christian persuasion. (See Appendix on page 108), "The Meeting between Theodore Beza and St. François de Sales." George Herbert, who in his *Passio Discerpta* had put the devotional techniques of the Catholic Reformation to some experimental use,[8] would certainly be open to engaging the impassioned spiritual advice and plenitude of sacred anecdote offered in St. François's *Introduction to the Devout Life*. Here I will examine one apparent instance of Herbert reconstituting an insight presented in the French devotional work, a vignette that emerges in the thirteenth chapter of the Second Part of the *Introduction* in the context of explaining "*aspirations, jaculatory prayers, and good thoughts*" (p. G12^v). St. François attempts here to show how lovers of God are spontaneously aroused to holy

---

that evidence printed since Hutchinson's time has shown that Henry "had been in Paris at least as early as 1615, perhaps 1614"; and that "if the brother mentioned in the second postscript is Edward, the date may be late 1616 or early 1617"; see *A Life of George Herbert* (Ithaca, NY: Cornell University Press, 1977), pp. 75, 83–84. The first English translation of St. François's manual was published in 1613, and by 1614 three editions of the translation had been printed; see *Introduction*, p. 10.

8 Clarke, pp. 78–79.

thoughts in passing worldly circumstances and through encounters with natural phenomena. In one offered example of such behavior, de Sales recalls that

> S. Basil the great sayth, that the rose among the thornes & briers, seemeth to make this exhortation to men. *Whatsoever is most pleasant in this world, ô mortal men, is entermingled with sorow: nothing is pure and unmixed: griefs be always companions of myrth, and widdowhead of mariage, and care of education is joined with fertility & aboundance of children, shame folows glory, expences waite upon honours, disgust is the sauce of delicate dishes, and sicknes pue-felow of health. A fair flower is the rose* (sayth this holy man) *but yet it filleth me with sadnes, putting me in mind of my sinne, for which the earth hath been condemned to bring foorth thornes and bryers* (pp. H4^r-H4^v).

This is one of many references in an expansive and seemingly fortuitous series of sacred insights: St. Anselm compares the flight of the hare to the soul under the constraints of sin; St. Fulgentius appreciates that the glories of heaven will be even greater than impressive noble attire in the courts of kings; St. Francis Borgia contrasts the obedience of trained falcons with man's unruliness; and St. Basil relays the sermon of the rose, yet another devout response to everyday sights and encounters. In *The Temple*, by contrast, the teaching rose becomes part of a combative debate, a reply to a secular counterpart who would challenge the subjection of worldly goods to balanced and cautious limitations established by Herbert earlier in his lyric sequence.[9]

> Presse me not to take more pleasure
> In this world of sugred lies,
> And to use a larger measure
> Than my strict, yet welcome size. (ll. 1–4)

Herbert counters his opponent's advocacy of worldly pleasures with three arguments for avoiding any pursuit of secular goods at all. The

---

[9] Most notably, in his poem "The Size" (137–138), to which l. 4 of "The Rose" briefly refers.

first two are simple objections that prepare the way for the poem's central rhetorical strategy.

> First, there is no pleasure here:
> > Colour'd griefs indeed there are,
> Blushing woes, that look as cleare
> > As if they could beautie spare.
>
> Or if such deceits there be,
> > Such delights I meant to say;
> There are no such things to me,
> > Who have pass'd my right away. (ll. 5–12)

Worldly goods are "Colour'd griefs" and "Blushing woes": Herbert would seem to collapse St. Basil's sequence of pairs—"*widdowhead*" with "*marriage*," "*care of education*" with "*aboundance of children*," "*shame*" with "*glory*"—into nouns with spurious adjectives; and he makes it clear that even referring to secular "delights" can only be justified in terms of his current audience. He has passed away his right to secondary goods by accepting other goods offered in the life to come. Herbert does not however rest his case on these initial arguments, but moves to engage his opponent with what might be taken as a gesture of worldly rapprochement: he will offer him a flower!

> But I will not much oppose
> > Unto what you now advise:
> Onely take this gentle rose,
> > And therein my answer lies. (ll. 13–16)

Here at the center of the poem, the main image appears, already signaled by the title and suggested by the paradoxical "Colour'd griefs" and "Blushing woes"; and it seems for a moment that the speaker has indeed changed his mind about the goods "that worldlings prize," that he "will not much oppose" celebrating them, and that he has decided "to take more pleasure / In this world": "What is fairer than a rose? / What is sweeter?" he intones. Of course, this is actually a concession for rhetorical effect, and the homily delivered by Herbert's rose turns out to be rather more severe than the "objection" of St. Basil's. This flower is not a symbol of ephemeral good or of beauty that must wither, but rather a quick-acting and unpleasant medicine.

> What is fairer than a rose?
> What is sweeter? Yet it purgeth.
> Purgings enmitie disclose,
> Enmitie forbearance urgeth.
>
> If then all that worldlings prize
> Be contracted to a rose;
> Sweetly there indeed it lies,
> But it biteth in the close.
>
> So this flower doth judge and sentence
> Worldly joyes to be a scourge:
> For they all produce repentance,
> And repentance is a purge. (ll. 17–28)

Herbert's exposé on worldly joys does not pursue or even adapt the elegiac classical image of the rose's evanescence,[10] and it also sidelines the paradox of the rose's thorns, which the poem never mentions. Instead, Herbert steps through a logical diagnosis that focuses on the rose's predictable effect when ingested. Herbert's speaker closes his case and his response to his worldly interlocutor with a witty and ironic summary, capped with an elegant aesthetic equivocation.

> But I health, not physic choose:
> Onely though I you oppose,
> Say that fairly I refuse,
> For my answer is a rose. (ll. 29–32)

Herbert's "answer is a rose"—not only the flower beautifully and justly proffered and explained within the poem, but the poem itself as a literary artifact whose last word indicates the title—an artifact now humorously clarified in terms of its prospective effect. Certainly the attitude Herbert takes toward worldliness in this lyric is not inconsonant with de Sales's advisements, in the quotations from St. Basil and elsewhere in the *Introduction*,[11] but one notes an ascetic

---

10 Don Cameron Allen in *Image and Meaning: Metaphoric Traditions in Renaissance Poetry* (Baltimore, MD: Johns Hopkins University Press, 1960) mentions "the pagan and hence worldly transcription of the flower as a sign of human hopelessness and helplessness" (p. 68).

11 See, for instance, St. François's observations about how "we must not regard the scoffes and mocking taunts of the children of this world" in *Introduction*, pp. X1ʳ-X4ʳ.

personal engagement that one might specifically call Protestant when comparing St. Basil's general disenchantment with temporality in a fallen world to George Herbert's indictment of "all that worldlings prize" as a spiritual "scourge." Naturally, one need not presume that Herbert borrowed his proclamatory rose specifically from de Sales's *Introduction*, as the reference to St. Basil could be seen in any of various patristic assemblages where St. François probably saw it; and Herbert may also have constructed his own symbol independently in response to the widespread traditional uses of the rose as a symbol of worldly goods. But it seems quite likely that Herbert was aware of de Sales's citation of St. Basil, and his lyric "The Rose" does fashion in any case a bluff and humorous Anglican recast of his Gallic Romanist counterpart's *sic transit gloria mundi*.

The tacit awareness of continental devotion which many have detected in *The Temple* and George Herbert's evident interest in discreetly emulating, answering, and assimilating holiness from abroad can be seen largely to reflect the devotional practices of his friend and patron Lancelot Andrewes; and certainly Herbert's English poems have been experienced by many practicing Anglicans ever since their publication as an outworking, a personal lyric presentation, of the learned and ample spirituality associated with Andrewes, a bishop conscious of liturgies, missals, and primers ancient and modern, and one who prayed each Monday

>   For the Catholic Church,
>   its establishment and increase;
>   for the Eastern,
>   its deliverance and union;
>   for the Western,
>   its adjustment and peace;
>   for the British,
>   the supply of what is wanting in it,
>   the strengthening of what remains in it.[12]

Herbert's first generation of poetic followers generally encountered *The Temple* within this post-Hookerian Anglican context, and in no case more so than Henry Vaughan, who declared himself a pious

---

12 J. H. Newman, tr., *The Devotions of Bishop Andrewes*, vol. i. (London: S. P. C. K.; New York: Macmillan, 1920), p. 57. Andrewes's original Greek texts were first published in 1646.

convert of George Herbert's "holy *life* and *verse.*"[13] One observes however some remarkable differences between, on the one hand, Herbert's guarded, implicit responses to religious currents on the Continent and, on the other, Vaughan's active and public pursuit of a continental religious lineage, his translation and publication of poems and devotional treatises authored and edited by Polish, German, French, and Italian Jesuits,[14] and especially his spiritual and aesthetic self-modeling in response to the career of St. Paulinus of Nola, a Roman Senator and poet from Aquitaine who became an important figure in the earliest stages of western Christian monasticism, and whose pioneering work as a post-classical sacred poet had influence comparable to George Herbert's in the formation of Vaughan's sacred literary vision.[15] Vaughan seems to have known of Paulinus and his works even when he was pursuing his early poetic efforts as an occasional and classicist emulator of Ben Jonson and Thomas Randolph, but he also seems at first not to have been particularly attracted to Paulinus's vision. In one of his early classicist lyrics Vaughan presented himself as a literary descendant of Ausonius,[16] a Latin tutor and official who mentored Paulinus in classical poetry and opposed Paulinus's Christian asceticism. Vaughan translated Ausonius's humorous idyll describing an Elysium of women disappointed in love who attempt to retaliate by crucifying the god Cupid: in this poem's clouded underworld, "*griefe* and *absence* doe but *Edge* desire, / And Death is *fuell* to a Lovers *fire*" (210, ll.53–54). In the earliest stages of his career, Vaughan was thinking of death in secular and philosophical terms, as an acknowledged prospect signaling intensity in friendship or erotic love,[17] as an equalizer and a check on human

---

13 Donald R. Dickson, Alan Rudrum, and Robert Wilcher, eds., *The Works of Henry Vaughan* (Oxford: Oxford University Press, 2018), p. 558. References to Vaughan's works below will be cited by page or line within my text to this edition.

14 Translations from Casimir Sarbiewski's Odes appeared in *Olor Iscanus* (1651); works edited by Héribert Rosweyde and Fronton Le Duc, and authored by John Nieremberg and Francesco Sacchini, provided the originals for Vaughan's translations in *Flores Solitudinis* (1654).

15 See Jonathan Nauman, "Classicism and Conversion: The Role of the Poems and Letters of St. Paulinus of Nola in Henry Vaughan's *Silex Scintillans*," *Scintilla* 18 (2015): 13–26, for an account of Vaughan's access to St. Paulinus's texts and evidence for their influence in Vaughan's sacred verse.

16 See "To the River *Isca*," l. 7 (173).

17 See, for example, "To my Ingenuous Friend, R. W.," ll. 17–28 (12) and "UPON THE PRIORY GROVE, His usuall Retyrement," ll. 23–36 (25).

pride,[18] as a demonstration of valor,[19] but not with any focus on a Christian's passage "from this world of thrall / Into true liberty" (568, ll. 35–36). The actual death of Henry Vaughan's brother William in 1648 seems to have marked the beginning of a spiritual realignment in Vaughan's personal and literary life, such that Paulinus came to displace Ausonius as Vaughan's preferred literary ancestor.[20]

As with Paulinus, Vaughan seems to have known Herbert's works before acknowledging himself subdued by Herbert's "holy, ever-living lines,"[21] and his choice of a new continental and patristic

---

18 Vaughan learns in "The Charnel-house" to "season all succeeding Jollitie, / Yet damn not mirth, nor think too much is fit, / Excesse hath no *Religion*, nor *Wit*" (177, ll. 62–64).

19 See "an Elegie on the death of Mr. *R. W.*, slain in the late unfortunate differences at *Routon* Heath, neer *Chester*, 1645" (184–186), especially ll. 39–88. Christian expectations of personal resurrection are present but peripheral in this elegy, while "An Elegie on the death of Mr. *R. Hall*, slain at *Pontefract*, 1648" (193–195), written after Vaughan's brother's death, strongly subordinates military praise for the heroic soldier and clergyman to honoring his "*Piety* and *Learning*" (l. 55), and the poem's conclusion engages in a lengthy contemplation of Hall's spiritual ascent to heaven at his death (ll. 59–68). The change in tone between these two elegies seems to me to go beyond differences in personality between Vaughan's two heroic friends, and to reflect a strengthening of moral priorities in the author. One can observe a similar contrast between Vaughan's early commendation "Upon Mr. *Fletchers* Playes, published, 1647" (189–191) and his later commendation "To Sir *William D'avenant*, upon his *Gondibert*" (199–201); see Jonathan Nauman, "Toward a Herbertian Poetic: Vaughan's Rigorism and 'The Publisher to the Reader' of *Olor Iscanus*," *George Herbert Journal* 23 (Fall 1999/Spring 2000): 80–104. For the dating of R. Hall's death (October 1648) see F. E. Hutchinson, *Henry Vaughan: A Life and Interpretation* (Oxford: Clarendon Press, 1947), p. 61, n. 4.

20 Interestingly, Vaughan's decision to pursue his Christian religious commitment more rigorously, often called his conversion, seems itself to have been modeled in the life of Paulinus, who turned toward serious Christian observance in response to the unexpected death of a brother. See Nauman, "Classicism and Conversion," pp. 17–19.

21 See "The Match" (97, l. 1). Vaughan seems to have poetically absorbed Herbert's *The Temple* before his own spiritual vision aligned with Herbert's; see Jonathan Nauman, "'To my Worthy Friend Master *T. Lewes*': Vaughan, Herbert, and the Civil Wars," *Scintilla* 2 (1998): 128–131 for an analysis of one use of Herbert in *Olor Iscanus* that very likely preceded William's death and the religious seriousness that enabled *Silex Scintillans*. The sort of verbal borrowing without exact or attentive allusion practiced in "To my Worthy Friend" (196–197), in which ll. 38–40 and 45 quote from Herbert's "The Discharge" (144–145), can also be seen in non-devotional lyrics written during Vaughan's acknowledged discipleship under George Herbert; see "An Epitaph upon the Lady *Elizabeth*, Second Daughter to his late Majestie" (198–199), which quotes in ll. 13–14 from Herbert's "The Familie" (136–137) and in l. 21 from Herbert's "Confession" (126), and also "*To the pious*

model coincided with his much better known acceptance of a new English master for his "*life* and *verse*." But though Herbert's status as model for *Silex Scintillans* is explicit and, in terms of verbal borrowing unprecedented, Vaughan's decisive repudiation of his earlier classicist work in his 1654 Preface to *Silex Scintillans* derived more from his new sacred Latin allegiance than from his new English discipleship. One finds in the edition of Paulinus's works that Vaughan is known to have used[22] a letter written to Paulinus's Aquitainian kinsman Jovius, a literary man interested in Christianity but much involved in classical poetry and philosophy. This letter, evidently one of a series directed to Jovius, urges the latter to "put classical literature second to the Sacred Scriptures both in your judgment of their value and in your enthusiasm for them" (*ACW Letters I*, p. 157), making this point in the context of appreciating the real attraction Jovius feels toward classically trained eloquence. Paulinus carefully explains, in terms which seem to derive from his own spiritual and literary experience, that dedicating "your powers of mind and all the resources of intellect and tongue" to God will in fact bring the good results that classicist learning seeks; "As soon as you concentrate your mind's eye on the sanctuary above," Paulinus says, "Truth will reveal Its face to you and unlock to you your own person, because it is by recognition of the divine truth that we also come to know ourselves" (*ACW Letters I*, p. 160). One can see in this line of argument why Paulinus was a valued friend and correspondent of St. Augustine; but Paulinus's training and talent as a poet made him an especially effective advocate of Christianity for those like Jovius, as Paulinus was able to go beyond philosophical argument and demonstrate through poetic composition his imaginative enthusiasm for the Christian sacred. Thus he also sent to Jovius, as a follow-up to his

---

memorie of C. W. Esquire *who finished his Course here, and made his Entrance into Immortality upon the* 13 *of* September, *in the year of* Redemption 1653" (735–737), which quotes in ll. 59–60 from Herbert's "The H. Communion" (52–53). Similarly oblique borrowings from Herbert occur throughout Vaughan's sacred verse.

22 Héribert Rosweyde and Fronton Le Duc, eds., *Divi Paulini Episcopi Nolani Opera*, Antwerp: ex officinia Plantiniana, 1622. English translations of Paulinus's poems and letters in my text below are taken from P. G. Walsh, tr., *Letters of St. Paulinus of Nola*, vol. 1 [*Ancient Christian Writers*, vol. 35], Westminster, MD: The Newman Press; London: Longmans, Green and Company, 1968 and from P. G. Walsh, tr., *The Poems of St. Paulinus of Nola* [*Ancient Christian Writers*, vol. 40], New York and Ramsey, NJ: Newman Press, 1975. These translations will be cited in my text below as *ACW Letters I* and *ACW Poems*.

letter,[23] a poem in the classical *protreptikon* form,[24] exhorting Jovius in well-crafted verses with Virgilian allusions to redirect his poetic efforts toward sacred topics.

> Start to devote your heart solely to God's affairs. Raise your thoughts from earth and direct them up to God. Then before your eyes the sky will open and a new light will emerge. The Holy Spirit will enter with silent movement your hidden parts, and will rustle in your heart with His glad breath. Come now, wield your lyre, stir your fertile heart to essay a great theme; let that fluency devoted to your customary songs give place, for a greater sequence of topics is now inaugurated for you. Your theme is now not the judgment of Paris or the fictitious wars of the giants. True, this was your sport of old in your childhood days, for games were appropriate for a young child. But now that you are more advanced in years, and accordingly more serious in purpose, you must spurn with adult mind the unsubstantial Muses. You must take up subjects demanded by your age, for which chaste manners are now apposite, and by the venerable appearance of your countenance. You must conceive thoughts of God. (*ACW Poems*, p. 202)

Henry Vaughan followed Paulinus's advice in rechanneling his literary efforts toward Christian topics, and he relayed Paulinus's admonitions in his exhortations against "idle *Poems*" (555) in the 1654 Preface to *Silex Scintillans,* though in Vaughan's case the rejection of secular verse is more rigorous. This was because Vaughan's early literary tack had flirted with lower sorts of wit than those Paulinus associated with Jovius's "unsubstantial Muses." Vaughan had for instance read and absorbed Donne's scurrilous and pornographic Elegies[25]: probably these were some of the poems he had in mind

---

23 Echoes of the letter in the poem seem to imply that the two pieces were "written about the same time" (*ACW Poems*, p. 391), and in the Rosweyde-Le Duc edition they are printed together (pp. 342–357).

24 The *protreptikon*, "a work of exhortation or instruction" (*ACW Poems*, p. 391), had also been used by Cicero, and less seriously by Ausonius; see R. P. H. Green, *The Poetry of Paulinus of Nola: A Study of his Latinity* (Brussels: Latomus, 1971), pp. 38–39.

25 Vaughan interpolated lines from Donne's Fourth Elegy ("The Perfume") into his translation of Ausonius's Sixth Idyll (211, ll. 89–92; 1036).

when he denounced *"vitious verse"* and the use of "a *good* wit in a *bad* subject" (556)[26]; likely enough he had circulated some lewd emulations that were among the *"greatest follies"* which he testified to having suppressed (557). But amidst his stern denunciations of poets "wallowing in *impure thoughts* and *scurrilous conceits*" (556), Vaughan retained Paulinus's basic optimism about the worthiness of literary endeavor. Even those who misused their talents could relent and choose to produce "other Monuments of those excellent abilities conferred upon them" (555); and as Paulinus had intimated, it could fittingly be expected that youthful immaturity should give way to more serious pursuits "after years of discretion" (556). Vaughan's survey of literary corruption in himself and in others modulates finally into positive recommendations, rejecting censorship as an effective solution to literary immorality and espousing conversion instead: "the true remedy lies wholly in their bosoms, who are the gifted persons, by a wise exchange of *vain* and *vitious subjects*, for *divine Themes* and *Celestial praise*" (558). Here Vaughan makes his famous profession of discipleship under George Herbert, and immediately follows it with critical observations on earlier attempts to pursue *The Temple* as a poetic lead. While Paulinus had urged Jovius toward Christian poetic work on grounds that such endeavors would be life-transforming rather than mere literary exercises,[27] Vaughan urges similarly the importance of subordinating literary to spiritual motives even after accepting a sacred topic, attributing the failures of some of Herbert's followers to their aiming "more at *verse*, then *perfection*" (558). Other features of Paulinus's exhortations in his poem to Jovius also seem relevant and contributory to Vaughan's sacred stance in his poems and Preface. Paulinus's arguments favoring Christian over classical pagan cosmologies resonated with Vaughan's hermetic inclinations to connect science

---

26 When Vaughan's Preface renders Prudentius's denunciation of Symmachus for having "prophanely marr'd / A rich, rare stile with sinful, lewd contents," comparing Symmachus's performance with using "polish'd ivory" to "stir / A dirty sink," he remarks that "this *comparison* is nothing odious" (556), perhaps ironically echoing the last line of Donne's scurrilous Eighth Elegy ("The Comparison"), "She, and comparisons are odious." This gesture, if intended, would appositely implicate Donne's secular lyrics in Vaughan's arraignment. See C. A. Patrides, ed., *The Complete English Poems of John Donne* (London and Melbourne: J. M. Dent and Sons, 1985), pp. 149–152.

27 "How much greater fame will accrue for you from these themes which will not only exercise your tongue but will also inform your scrupulous mind, and from which you will obtain not only praise but also life!" (*ACW Poems*, p. 203).

with Holy Scripture; furthermore, while addressing cosmological issues, Paulinus had especially spotlighted miracles associated with the Biblical King Hezekiah (*ACW Poems*, p. 206), whose prayers and healing Vaughan takes in *Silex Scintillans* (1655) as a sacred antecedent to his own experience of sickness and divinely granted recovery.[28] Paulinus concludes his exhortations toward Jovius in terms both exalted and intimate:

> I beg you, devote your studies and efforts rather to reading and writing about these [sacred] events. ...
> Then I shall pronounce you truly a poet divinely inspired, and I shall drain your songs like a draught of sweet water, when they provide for me nectar from the heavenly fount as they sing of Christ the Lord of Creation and attest that your mind is potent with God. Thus I can obtain from you wealth of tongue and mind, and, already rejoicing to have you as kinsman by marriage, I will be able to felicitate you on being also akin to me in holy religion. The chains that bind us will not be loosed with our mortal bodies, and I will be able to embrace you with eternal pledges as my revered brother.
> Read this, Jovius, and blessings in Christ Jesus our Lord.
> (*ACW Poems*, pp. 207–208)

Vaughan closes his own recommendations to his fellow poets with similar challenge and anticipation:

> It is true indeed, that to give up our thoughts to pious *Themes* and *Contemplations* (if it be done for pieties sake) is a great *step* towards *perfection*; because it will *refine*, and *dispose* to devotion and sanctity. And further, it will *procure* for us (so easily communicable is that *loving spirit*) some small *prelibation* of those heavenly *refreshments*, which descend but seldom, and then very sparingly, upon *men* of an ordinary or indifferent *holyness*; but he that desires to excel in this kinde of *Hagiography*, or holy writing, must strive (by all means) for *perfection*

---

28 Philip West examines Vaughan's self-modeling after Hezekiah in *Henry Vaughan's* Silex Scintillans: *Scripture Uses* (New York: Oxford University Press, 2001), pp. 63–104.

and true *holiness*, that a door may be opened to him in heaven, Rev. 4.1. and then he will be able to write (with *Hierotheus* and holy *Herbert*) A *true Hymn*. (558)

The position George Herbert takes in Vaughan's summary statement here clearly indicates the pivotal importance of Vaughan's alignment with Paulinus in framing his way of reading and following Herbert, whom Vaughan perceived as "a companion to the primitive Saints"[29] in a manner probably beyond the expectations of Nicholas Ferrar writing for Herbert's Printers. The poet of "The British Church" had become the most recent representative of a continental line of Christian sacred poets ranging back to a contemporary of the Apostles whom Dionysius the Areopagite testified to having seen celebrating in divine praise at the Dormition of the Blessed Virgin.[30]

Like Lancelot Andrewes, Herbert considered it important for Anglicans to feel the presence of "a formal visible Church" behind them,[31] and episcopal Anglicans under the Commonwealth and Protectorate experienced *The Temple* as a continuing landmark for this traditional vision. Vaughan found in his new Herbertian poetic a replacement classicism aligned with the sacred poetic vision of St. Paulinus and rooted in an even more distant patristic past. That Herbert's verse could function as vitally as it did within this new context certainly testifies to the sacred artistic tact and achievement of *The Temple*.

---

29 *Works of George Herbert*, p. 3. For the development of Vaughan's image of Herbert in his prose publications, see Jonathan Nauman, "With Patriarchs and Prophets: Herbert in Vaughan's *Mount of Olives*" in Christopher Hodgkins, ed., *Locating George Herbert: Family, Place, Traditions* in *George Herbert Journal* 37, i/ii (2013/2014): 178–192.

30 See Colm Luibheid, tr., *Pseudo-Dionysius: The Complete Works* (New York and Mahwah, NJ: Paulist Press, 1987), p.84.

31 T. S. Eliot, *For Lancelot Andrewes: Essays on Style and Order* (London: Faber & Faber, [1928] 1970), p. 15.

Appendix

The Meeting between Theodore Beza and St. François de Sales

Historians writing from secular, Protestant, and Catholic angles have all found this well-attested 1597 incident uncomfortable and difficult to explain in a manner coherent with their own assumptions; see for example Henry Martyn Baird's Protestant account in *Theodore Beza: Counsellor of the French Reformation* (New York and London: G. P. Putnam's Sons, 1899), pp. 333–341, where François de Sales's mission work in the Chablais is characterized as follows:

It has been the boast of [de Sales's] friends and admirers, that by his instrumentality no fewer than seventy thousand Protestants, constituting almost the entire population of the district of Chablais, east and south of the Lake of Geneva, were brought into the bosom of the Roman Catholic Church. His methods have been represented as purely spiritual, inspired by love and carried out in gentleness. In reality they were an appeal to worldly considerations, backed by a display of military force and characterised by cruelties such as have rarely been exceeded in the history of religious intolerance.

This description of François's activities is not only impossible to sustain in reference to recent reviews of historical evidence connected with that mission, but sorts not at all with Beza's own willingness to treat with François. As Jill Fehleison has shown, François's movement in the Chablais certainly did not succeed in absence of what would tend now to be called culturally aggressive measures, including an influx of mission priests, organization of public displays of Catholic-oriented devotion, and the holding of demagogic public debates. But the movement featured only sporadic and ill-coordinated economic and political reinforcement from the Duke of Savoy: though a few Protestants were indeed driven from public office, Baird's reference to rarely-exceeded cruelties seems totally unaccountable; see Fehleison, *Boundaries of Faith: Catholics and Protestants in the Diocese of Geneva* (Kirkville, MO: Truman University Press, 2010), pp. 53–99. Baird professes himself unable to believe that Beza merely deflected François's arguments and offers of clemency and preferment from Rome with a calm affirmation "that the Roman church was [indeed] the mother Church, but ... that he did not despair of being saved in the religion wherein he was" (338–339); rather, Baird instructs his readers to reject the testimony of Auguste de Sales which his account has up to the point followed, in favor of "a Genevese manuscript" that claims Beza's final words to François were those of Christ to Peter (Mt. 16:23), "*Vade retro, Satanas!*" or else "an oral tradition" that renders a sarcastic conclusion: "Go sir, I am too old and deaf to be able to give ear to such words!" (339). However, these preferred shifts toward sharper dismissals seem merely to highlight the question of why Beza would not have said them earlier and preferably before the conversations even began. The *Catholic Encyclopedia*'s take on the Beza-de Sales encounter, appearing in an article on St. François by Raphael Pernin, falls similarly into evident errors and improbabilities. Pernin claims that "at the request of the pope, Clement VIII, [St. François] went to Geneva to interview Theodore Beza, who was called the Patriarch of the Reformation. The latter received him kindly and seemed for a while shaken, but had not the courage to take the final steps"; see *Catholic Encyclopedia*, vol. 6 (New York: Robert Appleton Company, 1909), p. 220. Recent attentions to the correspondences surrounding François's efforts indicate rather that the attempt to convert Beza was a plot hatched between François and Capuchin missionary Esprit de Beaume, with papal approval solicited as preparation for the endeavor (Fehleison, p. 62). Accounts characterizing Beza as "shaken" may well indicate that the thirty-year-old de Sales misinterpreted certain of his octogenarian interlocutor's courteous irenicisms, such as when the old Reformer said, "As for myself, if I am not in the right way I pray to God every day that He will lead me into it" (see Baird, p. 337). Pernin's concluding phrase, averring that Beza was convinced by François but lacked "courage to take the final steps," seems to portray Beza in a manner wildly out of character. The man who had recently faced down Protestant opponents on all sides to assert supralapsarian predestination at the Colloquy of Montbéliard (1586) and who openly confronted the French monarch Henri IV for accepting Catholicism (1593) was certainly not one to shrink from the public consequences of ideas he believed to be true. After François's visits in Geneva, rumors circulated claiming that Beza was converting, and the Reformer immediately responded with satirical polemics against the reports. Raphael Pernin and his twentieth-century editors cannot have been ignorant of this; and it is difficult to understand the *Encyclopedia*'s statements about this encounter as anything other than a partisan imposition.

An interesting and much more recent account of the meetings between Beza and de Sales can be found in Jill Fehleison's historical monograph *Boundaries of Faith*, cited above. Fehleison's secular academic approach enables a much more careful survey of the successful re-Catholicizing of the Chablais and of de Sales's unsuccessful efforts to persuade Beza, but aspects of the latter event remain puzzling to her: "in the end de Sales was unable to convince Beza to convert, but his easy entrée to the city and access to Beza are striking, and one wonders why the Reformed pastor was willing to meet with de Sales" (p. 63). Perhaps some answer to Fehleison's query can be made in terms of a wise remark from her monograph's introduction: "downplaying genuine religious motivation independent of larger institutions in a time period when belief was fundamental to identity shortchanges a crucial component of the early modern world" (p. 14). It is quite likely that Beza did not view young de Sales merely as a representative of the Roman Catholic faction. This energetic priest was a man attempting to serve Christ, and he was in many ways remarkably similar to Beza himself, a legal trainee with talent as a writer, who discovered a religious vocation in the context of a personal crisis over the doctrine of predestination. Beza probably considered the possibility that the Holy Spirit would use their conversations to bring de Sales out of his entanglements with the perceived worldlinesses of Rome. Fehleison (p. 63) states that the timing of the rumors of Beza's conversion indicate that they were caused not by a Jesuit plot (a common Protestant suggestion then and since), but by Beza's willingness to hold the meetings at all. It is likely that Beza knew the risk and was willing to take it, accurately feeling that he would be quite capable of answering any such false reports.

Madeira Forest
by David Brown

THOR BACON

Little Fugue on the Hands

You move like the wings of a junkyard angel,
opening like autumn, making me forget
if I'm a sapling birch,
or a sunning painted turtle.
You woo
the spoon from maple wood, charm
the vase from spinning clay, chase
the ivy's verb along the leather scabbard.
A mother with five children,
your speech uncoils like the creek's fingerprints
where the whorled willow grows.
How may we read
your touch
except with wakened skin?
I gaze at your knuckly mountains, doze
in the valley of your cupped palms, wondering,
by middle age,
which Commandment we haven't broken.
Yet you've stayed loyal all through it all,
faithful sisters,
witness to my many failures,
my few victories,
pair of otters,
pearl earrings,
perfect ten,
here with me as I close the notebook,
two cats purring on my lap.

Mowing After a Week of Rain

I pause at the little peach up front –
no scent left in the few clinging blossoms.
Later, spewing
sheared blades against the back fence, I notice
the columbine flowers in the corner shriveling,
rumpled jesters' hats
the morning after a royal feast.
Nearby, tulip skirts lie on the garden floor.
How did I miss it all?
What pursuit was worthier?
Listen, you who breathed us all awake –
don't bother with a Paradise that leaves any of them out.

MARTIN BENNETT

Above the Forum

Though marked before by Gibbon then Goethe
How moonlight like some spectral weight-lifter
Shifts arch, porch, cornice and architrave –

Between first century and 2019AD
Their mass appears to hang by an eyelid,
Brick reticulum made feathery, marble

Or travertine defiantly afloat; soil-
bound archaeology is rendered
Metaphysical. This a footnote from on high.

Tropical Stopover

Cotonou. République Populaire du Benin

Politics a game of volleyball with a too high net,
The town wraps all in hospitable smallness. Round as day,
Sea's a diamond factory no boss can fathom.
Along the front the flags are genies dancing
Or are they soldiers vanished in a mirage of laughter
Now sky beats invisible blue drums to celebrate
New Year arriving on the next down-breeze?

Further inland the hats are the colour of rainbows.
Wine and sunlight make even the policemen friendly.
Masks, stilt-jacks, tam-tams unlock closenesses that are
Everyday's subconscious sadly hidden from itself. Aeeeiii!
All at once the air is alive with vowels. There,
Whistling the latest samba from Brazil, strolls Monsieur Zephyr
In indigo bowler and flowing iridescent tails.
The sun blows while waves, tirelessly-elbowed, clash cymbals.
Downtown saxophones rip bumphous doldrums to welcome shreds.

But look. La Place de l'Etoile Rouge is putting on her necklace.
Salut, tous mes camarades, I must be leaving –
Tomorrow I shall carry your memory like a postcard one consults
When elsewhere gets overbearing, an amulet, however small,
Once back in zones and nations for which time's as tight as thimbles,
With faces of gigantic stone that have forgotten how to smile.

JEREMY HOOKER

A philosopher in search of the soul

1
He sits in his study, books
and computer on his desk, while
Plato's chariot races through his mind.

Dark horse, light horse –
                        how they scatter
thought – a tumult of reason
and desire, which, momentarily,
Aristotle calms, restoring soul
to the body's shape.

Now old Yeats disturbs his calm.
What am I, he thinks, if not
                        a paltry thing,
a scarecrow with a tattered book,
or as the learned fool has said,
a piece of cosmic scum?

2
Head on the desk, he sleeps,
and dreams a Cookham dream
of tombs prized open
where the new-hatched dead
rise up, dazed with surprise.
They shake off dust, and climbing
to the light, resume their lives.

3
He wakes to thoughts
of parents, lover, friends –
a cloud in which each face appears.
Do they dissolve, from being
into nothingness?
A whisper in his ear:
'To philosophise
is to learn to die'.
A sudden wind storms
through the room,
tearing pages from his books.
He is alone, his study scattered
to the elements – a man exposed
upon an inner shore,
that fronts an outer tide.

4
Grief is the sea
that sends a shockwave to his heart.
    Where is the life
that I saw die from the beloved eyes?
              Gone,
for ever gone,
Anima, breath of life,
             no word
can tell me what I seek,
no image and no shade.
What lasts is memory,
which is an inner sea, now
calm, now storming at the walls of sense
but never still until I die.

ISABEL BERMUDEZ

Spring wood

Bracken dries,
crackles

and hisses: a log
that burns and spits.

Alarm in the trees:
the years disturbed

by scurrying
and birdsong,

a chasing of tails
erupting then dying:

small fires spread
in the synapses –

trace and trail,
sun-light through calyces –

dead leaves from 1917:
the brown parcel-paper

of war-time
and Spanish flu.

At the base
of a beech

whose purplish knees
scrape the ground,

white anemones'
slight corpses

have sprung,
alive as light

from their winter's traps.

Honesty

It sprouts in clusters,
tumble-down belfries
high on the hills;

silvers
to a timpane membrane,
to ground frost.

Echo of bells
tolling throughout Spain
like a great sea
that is the heart,
churning.

Rattle of saucepans
and banging of lids,

clapping on doorsteps
and balconies.

A trail in the air
come evening:

weed,
self-seeded
and shriven,
blown in from the lane.

RACHEL CARNEY

Legerdemain

here you are
in front of me   a white rabbit from my hat
I reach out   fingers in the empty air

grasping at shadows   fool for a trick
I turn back   fix my eyes ahead and
here you are

in a burst of smoke
grinning like a clown   juggling so
I reach out   fingers scrabbling the air

feeling my way through the haze
following the echo of your voice and
here you are

again   dealing your cards face down
switching them around   so fast I can't see but
I reach out   fingers in mid-air

clutching at nothing   at where you should be
stumbling through the maze to you   and
here you are again
I reach out   fingers drift through air

SARAH LINDON

Present tense

Sun becomes blaze storms
darkly over standing water
catching again and again
where skating insects jump
while the burnished lilies
cup dank air like long-aged liquor,
steadying themselves grandly
as new-polished furniture.
Giant rhubarbs stretch shades
wide and canvas-thick and fine
sapphire pencil-leads drop
for rest on the rough hide
then whir off on clear, feather-light
chopsticking wings scissoring
the air in wordless shimmers.
Stories here are layers, all
present tense, beginning,
middle and end looking
straight at each other in every
direction. Just the earth's filigree
exoskeleton or air's various
excretions. Ferns tune
on the stream's damp breath,
their fanned ribs uncurl
fossil-script alveoli,
tiny, tough, reptilian, green.

I forget but nothing else does

The palm blades trim the air
a lampshade contains the light
a tilted smile of sand lazes
in the hourglass almost as if
wryly responding to my look –
we have been here all along –
while even as I have been
self-evidently living I have
stopped holding life and left
it in the windowpanes, chair,
some books, the darkness that still
takes and cools each day and
weighs it, so as to hand it back
with the right degree of change.
I wonder if this fierce, adamant
remembering of the world by
itself is what is meant by grace.

PETER LIMBRICK

Lizard

I am becoming reptile.
Skin drying to scales,
toenails hardening to claws.

A propensity for lying still,
belly slack.

Warm when the sun shines,
cold when it doesn't.

Mouth a toothless gape.

I flick my tongue over ice-cream
thinking nothing.

ROSIE JACKSON

Thinking of Simone Weil

French mystic, philosopher and political activist Simone Weil (1909–1943), developed a mathematical model to defend the value of 'affliction' as a way of attaining God.

I keep coming back to her, as if she might know how to dress
our current wounds, might reveal who cast the first stone.
I imagine meeting with her in Kent, that last year of her life,
Lyons corner house perhaps, the windows steamy, streets of
    Ashford
pelted with war-time rain. Her wire-rimmed spectacles
seem to see through things, and she pushes away the cake I buy,
her body thin as a key. How tongue-tied I feel with my questions
about her time on the front line in Spain, factory work at Renault's,
and what was it like, knowing Simone de Beauvoir? But she's
    beyond
all that now, sits as if the muggy cafe is a church, our two solitudes
candles waiting to be lit. Sits as if she shares the loneliness God
    carries,
the vast damp weight of it, and when I go for the ultimate riddle,
ask if suffering is the *only* gateway to God, if *malheur*
could not give way – on occasions, birthdays perhaps – to *joy*
as the passport to divine perfection, she looks over my shoulder,
as if there stands the more enlightened version of myself
she would far rather meet. She's been quizzed this way
many times before, her face full of sad knowing, absorbing
grief and ignorance much as a tree tries to turn the world
back to green. But where is divine love in all this, I want to know,
surely we're not here just to weep? Yes, there's war right now,
there's always wretchedness somewhere, but aren't we allowed
to enjoy ferns and wrens and apple blossom, aren't we allowed
the compensations – friendship, *absinthe*, music, sex, sleep?
Aren't we allowed *this*? I gesture to the rationed food, the chatter.
She smiles then, not the grim pride of a martyr, but the lucent gold
of a saint, a soul, perhaps, who stood once as a woman at the foot
of a cross, pained beyond measure to witness someone they love

suffer and suffer. Then, seeing that I think I've got the clue I came
    for,
she stands, leans towards me briefly. 'Don't make that mistake,' she says, against the clatter of teacups. 'Don't think it's about Him alone. It's not. It's Love. It's everyone.' And she walks out slowly into the rain. She's thirty-four, stepping into her final days the way she once entered the huge Abbey at Solesmes, its tall stone walls an ark against a flood, her starving body a white stick tapping its way home through the glorious absolving dark.

Review: Thomas Dilworth, *David Jones: Engraver, Soldier, Painter, Poet* (London: Jonathan Cape; Berkeley, CA: Counterpoint, 2017). £21.25.

GREG MILLER

David Jones was praised enthusiastically and publicly in his own day by W. H. Auden, T. S. Eliot, W. B. Yeats, Igor Stravinsky, Kenneth Clark, W. S. Merwin, and Basil Bunting, among others. Thomas Dilworth has given us our best literary biography to date of this master maker in *David Jones: Engraver, Soldier, Painter, Poet*. One can hope that Dilworth's biography, the fruit of decades of scholarship, will bring new readers to an artist who had very little interest in fame. Dilworth's exploration of the connections between Jones's visual art and poetry is new and illuminating. This biography serves both as an invitation to those who have not yet read Jones and as an invaluable resource to those who already know him.

William Blake, Dilworth tells us, was Jones's most admired model, and Jones's father, the evangelizing Nonconformist Welshman, preached on the same fields where "Blake had seen a tree spangled with angels" (9). Jones's mother had Anglo-Catholic sympathies, with "sacramental and Catholic notions" (32). Dilworth's biography permits a clearer understanding of the religious forces behind Jones's prodigious creativity: his wedding of Nonconforming Welsh zeal with a Catholic convert's passion. Jones's belief in the sacred nature of human making, in the sacramental sign and all makers of signs, has transformed and will continue to transform many, not only those who share his creed.

Dilworth's lifetime labour offers us a life of astonishingly textured particularity. Thom Gunn's "The Dump" describes what for Gunn would be a nightmare of biographical minutiae threatening to drown "the crisp vehemence / of a lifetime reduced to / half a foot of shelf space" (ll. 2–4). Dilworth's literary biography unfolds from different assumptions about the distinctions between art and life; he aims to give us Jones's inner weather, beginning with his formative psycho-sexual development, as much as it can be reconstructed. We learn that at the age of fourteen, for example, Jones was circumcised to address what he had described to his nurse as painful erections. His healing was slowed and marred, his erections painfully breaking the sutures.

Jones endured other traumas. As a child, David fought with his older brother Harold over the affections of his parents, learning to draw his mother's special attention, Dilworth argues, through sickness. Harold died of tuberculosis at 21, when David was an adolescent, after which the younger brother was "free," Dilworth argues, "of residual sibling rivalry" (24). An accident Jones suffered after that death Dilworth reads as caused by unconscious guilt (24). Dilworth reads as caused by unconscious guilt (24). *In Parentheses* reenacts his brother's death (242). The psychiatrist William A. H Stevenson's prescriptions left Jones drug addicted, seriously hampering his creativity for more than a decade. Whatever one makes of Dilworth's psychological analyses, Jones the poet and man took such delving into one's purported unconscious drives and motives seriously, though the effect on his own life appears to have been anything but salutary.

Much of this biography's psychological analysis is compelling and original—some is less so. Dilworth reads an important self-portrait that includes the artist only from the waist-up as a form "castration": "This is the altar of art, at which the artist in the mirror is sacrificed and reconstituted" (104). Jones is described as part of the 1% of the population on the Meyers-Briggs scale who are "introverted, intuitive, thinking and perceiving" (183). Not all readers will find such diagnoses and categorizations convincing or useful.

Though no Jones scholar, I must register a reservation. In his discussion of Jones's mentor Eric Gill, Jones's fiancée Petra Gill (Eric Gill's daughter), and the larger community of makers to which Jones attached himself, Dilworth is silent about Gill's apparent sexual relationship with Petra, commented upon by her and strangely attributed by another biographer to Gill's high sex drive. There is some evidence that later in life Jones was aware of this affair. Why, then, is there no mention in this psychologizing biography of what must have felt a betrayal? If Jones never confronted his mentor, what toll might his silence have exacted? And Dilworth's narrative drives home the extent to which the poet-artist was betrayed repeatedly and deeply by those he trusted. Late in life, for example, Dilworth argues that Jones's agent Saunders Lewis stole from him and engaged in "petty treachery" (346).

Dilworth questions Jones's trust in himself in matters of love and sex. He describes in detail a pattern of romantic disappointment and unrequited longing. Jones's first love, we read, was the nurse Elsie Hancock, to whom he wrote letters and sent drawings during the war. She answered with photographs. The romance went no further. Jones's last great infatuation was with the much younger Valerie Price, to whom he sent flowers and love letters, and whom he desired sexually and longed to marry, he told his friend Harman Grisewood in a letter (300). Dilworth speculates about a primal Freudian wound at the root of this lifelong pattern of disappointment. He also tells us Jones decided not to marry Petra because he could not support a family financially, choosing instead loyalty to his vocation: poetry and art. Whether or not a necessary renunciation, his celibacy proved painful.

Jones's renunciation was a choice made in the name of his art, his making of paintings, sculptures, and poems. (Fenton Johnson's recent *At the Center of All Beauty: Solitude and the Creative Life* is well worth reading on this topic.) Jones's passion for making is most clearly expressed in his book of essays, *Epoch and Artist*. These essays remain our best introduction to Jones as an artist. One need not share his Roman Catholicism or Welsh roots to be moved. Jones drew inspiration from Jessie Weston's *From Ritual to Romance* and Frazer's *The Golden Bough*. Initially disturbed by commonalities between Christian and pre-Christian mythology, Jones came in time to see the latter as part of divine providence. Jones's own myth-making, however, was unique. He imagined time as fluid, the Eucharist breaking and transforming reality.

> Heading toward, right astride
> To one degree beyond
>   Ffraid Santes' fire-track
> Where Brendon shall cry from his sea-horse
> *Mirabilis Deus in sanctis suis!*
>
> From before all time
>   the New Light beams for them
> and with eternal clarities
>   *infulsit* and athwart
> the fore-times.

And later in the same section, we read,

>   From before time
> his perpetual light
>   shines upon them.
>   Upon all at once
>   upon each one
>   whom he invites, bids, us to recall
>   when we make the recalling of him
>   daily, at the Stone.

The Incarnation, Crucifixion, and Resurrection alter time, rendering all holy. *The Anathemata* begins: "the holy and venerable hands lift up an efficacious sign."

This idea of the consecration of signs is central to Jones's thinking. He wrote his clarifying essays on this subject in *Epoch and Artist* reluctantly, Dilworth tells us, and was surprised and pleased by their favorable reception. (These key essays are not discussed in depth in this biography.) For Jones, gratuitous making, the sheer joy of creation beyond utility or function, defines us. To make symbols is to offer up dedicatory gifts to the gods, "anathemata," in praise of the gods. Symbol-makers by nature, poets and artists serve priestly functions. "But I here confine my use of the word to those artifacts in which there is an element of the extra-utile and the gratuitous. If there is any evidence of this kind of artefacture then the artifacturer or artifex should be regarded as participating directly in the benefits of the Passion, because the extra-utile is the mark of man" (*Anathemata* note, 65). For Jones, one need not share a sacramental understanding of art to take part in a sacrament.

The Anathemata is narrated by a Welshman taking Roman Catholic communion (with an interrupting passage narrated by the ancient figure of London herself) while meditating on history. The work is often compared with Joyce's *Finnegan's Wake*, which Jones revered. (Jones began and then put down Pound's *Cantos* out of fear of influence.) My experience of reading *The Anathematic* is more akin to what I feel reading Faulkner's *The Sound and the Fury*. I have to give up my bearings to find my way. I re-read in order to read, each experience distinctive, in order to apprehend the arc of the whole as well as the particular layered musicality of each moment of lyric consciousness. T. S. Eliot, Dillworth reminds us, recommended reading the book at least three times.

Not all readers will feel called to or rewarded by such reading. And Jones's politics remain a major impediment. Dilworth attempts to thread the needle for us. Like many in the 1930s who had survived the First World War, Jones favored appeasement to avoid war. Jones had grown up in a "Kipling-conditioned world," as he once put it, watching the City Imperial Volunteers march by his house during the Boer War in 1900. The memory called him as a young man to enlist in the Royal Welsh Infantry; he "believed 'the old lie'" (44). His disenchantment after the war was profound.

In time Jones became pro-Franco and anti-Republican. Jones associated Jews, Dilworth tells us, "with the business world, which he detested" (201) and argued that the fascists "deserve sympathy" (205); "he did not ... change his view about the basic accuracy of Hitler's critique of Western cultural decadence" (234). (Those interested in more primary evidence of Jones's thinking here may consult *David Jones on Religion, Politics, and Culture: Unpublished Prose* [Bloomsbury 2018], which includes his prewar thinking on Hitler.) Jones disliked the nascent European Union. He wished to limit immigration from Asia and Africa to preserve Britain's ability to assimilate immigrants (342). To democracy Jones preferred an idealized feudal monarchy (202). He dismissed Liberalism in favor of a "rightist Catholic European style" (125).

Despite his devotion to tradition and authority, Jones's Roman Catholicism did not toe the party line. He loathed the Council of Trent for its breaks from Catholic Tradition (127), he dismissed Roman Catholic injunctions against extramarital sexual activity, he condemned Pope Pius XII's attacks on modernism and evolution, and well before Vatican II gave him license greeted the idea that there is no salvation outside the church as nonsense. When Jones confessed to a priest that he had missed the previous Sunday mass and was warned that in doing so he had risked damnation, Jones rebuked the priest in strong terms.

Dilworth's biography gives us a strong sense of the man who wrote the poems and painted the paintings. We also see the arc of Jones's career. The biography describes artistic breakthroughs, situating them personally and historically. Dilworth argues, for example, that in 1925 Jones made a great leap in his painting. His "style becomes his own," (92) and he chose to burn many of his earlier sketches. Much later in his career, freed from prescribed medications after the death of his psychiatrist, Jones was able to compose *The Sleeping Lord* and *The Book of Balaam's Ass*, even though the *Kensington Mass* was left unfinished.

Dilworth presents us with an artist perpetually in resurrection, recovering from betrayal and the depression and anxiety resulting only in part from trench warfare. His poems will find their readers, just as his paintings have begun to find and transform their viewers. And for this reader, the poetry can and must be read against itself; the "old lie" threatens us again in many forms, as it threatened Jones, and the life and life's work give us delight and instruction, models of enchantment and disenchantment.

CONTRIBUTORS

AMANDA ATTFIELD lives in Herefordshire. Her poetry has appeared in anthologies, small presses and magazines. A mixed media artist, performer, and former member of The Border Poets, she was long-listed for the National Poetry Competition in 2017.
Instagram: @attfielda

THOR BACON's chapbook, *Making the Shore*, won the 2018 Red Dragonfly Press award. Holding a BA in Creative Writing from Antioch College he works as a jeweller in Michigan, USA. Recent poems in *The St. Katherine Review*, *Amethyst Review*, and *The Aurorean*.

MARTIN BENNETT lives in Rome where he teaches and contributes occasional articles to *Wanted in Rome*.

ISABEL BERMUDEZ lives in Orpington, Kent. Her latest collection is *Serenade* (Paekakariki Press, Walthamstowe, 2020). *Madonna Moon* won the Coast to Coast to Coast pamphlet prize in 2018. Two full collections with Rockingham Press. More at www.isabel-bermudez.com

RACHEL CARNEY is a poet and PhD student based in Cardiff. Her poems, reviews and articles have been published in several magazines including the *New Welsh Review*, *Acumen* and *Envoi*. Two of her poems have been shortlisted for the Bridport Prize.

PAUL CONNOLLY's poems have appeared in *Agenda*, *Poetry Salzburg*, *Takahē*, *FourXFour*, *Sarasvati*, *Envoi*, *The High Window*, *Eunoia Review*, *The Honest Ulsterman*, and will soon be published in *Quadrant*, *Stand Magazine* and *Chiron Review*.

PATRICK DEELEY has published seven collections with Dedalus Press, the latest *The End of the World* received the 2019 Lawrence O'Shaughnessy Award. He has recently had poems in *The London Magazine*, *SurVision*, *The Manoa Journal*, and in *Staying Human*, an anthology edited by Neil Astley.

ROGER GARFITT's latest collection is *The Action* (Carcanet, 2019). His memoir, *The Horseman's Word*, is a Vintage paperback and a CD of Poetry & Jazz is available from www.restringingthelyre.wordpress.com

SAM GARVAN has had work published in anthologies and journals including, most recently, *The French Literary Review*, *Ink*, *Sweat & Tears*, *Impossible Archetype* and *Acumen*. He works for a London beekeeper.

TOM GOUTHWAITE grew up in Yorkshire. A natural scientist and keen apprentice of the unknown, he has studied widely in the Kagyu Lineage of Tibetan Buddhism.

MICHAEL HENRY lives in Cheltenham and his latest publication was *The Bureau of the Lost and Found* with Five Seasons Press. He is currently putting together a Selected with some new work.

GRAHAM HIGH has simultaneously followed a career as a poet and as a visual artist (painter and sculptor). He has had six poetry collections published to date by various publishers. Website: www.grahamhigh.info

JEREMY HOOKER's most recent books are *Selected Poems 1965–2018* and *Art of Seeing: Essays on Poetry, Landscape Painting and Photography*, both published by Shearsman.

RIC HOOL's 10th collection of poetry *Personal Archaeology* (2020) is thematically centred on Cullercoats & Northumberland, his home for many years. A collaboration with artist Tim Rossiter, *Containing Multitudes*, based on the Ceridwen/Gwion Bach story, is due September 2021.

EVE JACKSON lives in Lee on Solent and is a Frogmore Poetry prize winner, a recent Featured Poet with Orbis and continues to be widely published in journals.

ROSIE JACKSON won 1st prize Poetry Teignmouth 2021. *Two Girls and a Beehive: Poems about Stanley Spencer*, co-written with Graham Burchell, and *Aloneness is a Many-headed Bird*, co-written with Dawn Gorman, appeared in 2020. www.rosiejackson.org.uk

PETER LIMBRICK is an educationalist interested in babies who have neurological impairment. He aspires to a Buddhist view of life and death.

SARAH LINDON's poems have appeared in magazines including *Agenda*, *Magma*, *Oxford Poetry*, *Poetry Wales*, *Scintilla*, *Stand*, *The Frogmore Papers*, and *The Reader*. She has an MPhil in Writing from the University of Glamorgan, and lives and works in London.

CONTRIBUTORS

GREG MILLER is Professor Emeritus of English, Millsaps College. He has recently published with Catherine Freis their third volume of translations and commentary: *George Herbert's Latin Prose: Orations and Letters* (George Herbert Journal Monograph Series). Greg is co-editor with Anne-Marie Miller-Blaise of a forthcoming collection of essays: *Edward Herbert and George Herbert in the European Republic of Letters* (Manchester University Press).

JONATHAN NAUMAN, Secretary of the Vaughan Association in North America, served on the editorial board for the new Oxford *Works of Henry Vaughan*. He is co-editor for the Association's forthcoming volume *Borderlands: The Art and Scholarship of Louise Imogen Guiney*.

CHRISTOPHER NORRIS is Emeritus Professor of Philosophy at Cardiff University. He has authored or edited over thirty books on philosophy, literary theory, intellectual history and music. Published eight volumes of poetry and philosophical verse. *As Knowing Goes and Other Poems* (Parlor Press) will appear later this year.

HELEN OVERELL lives in the Mole Valley and has published in magazines and anthologies. Her publications include *Inscapes & Horizons* (St Albert's Press, 2008), *Thumbprints* (Oversteps Books, 2015) and *Measures for lute* (The Lute Society, 2020).

LESLEY SAUNDERS has published several books of poems, most recently *Nominy-Dominy* (Two Rivers Press 2018). *Point of Honour*, an anthology of her translations of the acclaimed Portuguese poet Maria Teresa Horta, came out in 2019.

CLAIRE SCOTT is an award winning poet who has received multiple Pushcart Prize nominations. Claire is the author of *Waiting to be Called* and *Until I Couldn't*. She is the co-author of *Unfolding in Light: A Sisters' Journey in Photography and Poetry*.

JOCK STEIN is a piper and preacher from East Lothian, whose most recent books are *Swift* and *The Iolaire*, and a book of poetry and conversation, *From Ruth to Lamentations*. He has just completed a PhD at Glasgow University with a thesis on 'Temple and Tartan: The Psalms and Scotland'.

MATTHEW STEWART works in the Spanish wine trade and lives between West Sussex and Extremadura. Following two pamphlets with HappenStance Press, he published his first full collection, *The Knives of Villalejo*, in 2017. More recent work has appeared in *The Spectator*.

WILLIAM TATE, (Ph.D., The University of North Carolina at Chapel Hill) is Professor of English and Dean of Arts and Letters at Covenant College. His essays on Richard Wilbur, Martin Heidegger, and Jean-Luc Marion (among others) have appeared in *Christian Scholars Review*, *Christianity and Literature*, *Janus Head*, and *Logos: A Journal of Catholic Thought and Culture*.

SUSAN WALLACE is a writer and academic. She has worked in India, Malaysia, Greece and Italy. Her poems have been published in a range of journals and anthologies; and, as a member of the group, Hexameter, she occasionally performs her poetry to live audiences.

PHILIP WEST is Associate Professor of English at the University of Oxford. He has published articles on Vaughan and other early modern devotional writers, and his book *Scripture Uses: Henry Vaughan's 'Silex Scintillans'* (OUP, 2001) explores Vaughan's engagement with the Bible in the context of the Civil Wars. Currently he is completing a critical edition of the poems of James Shirley, and editing Vol. VI of *The Oxford Edition of the Sermons of John Donne*.

ROBERT WILCHER was Reader in Early Modern Studies in the English Department at the University of Birmingham until his retirement in 2007. His recent publications include *Henry Vaughan and the Usk Valley* (Logaston Press, 2016), edited with Elizabeth Siberry; *The Works of Henry Vaughan* (Oxford University Press, 2018), edited with Alan Rudrum and Donald Dickson; and *Keeping the Ancient Way: Aspects of the Life and Work of Henry Vaughan (1621–1695)* (Liverpool University Press, 2021).

CHARLES WILKINSON's poetry collections include the pamphlet *Ag & Au* (Flarestack, 2013) and *The Glazier's Choice* (Eyewear, 2019). He lives in Powys, Wales. Website: http://charleswilkinsonauthor.com/

MARGARET WILMOT settled in Sussex in 1978. She has been published in various British poetry magazines. Smiths Knoll published a pamphlet *Sweet Coffee* in 2013. *Man Walking on Water with Tie Askew*, a full-length book of poems, was published by The High Window in June 2019.

JONATHAN WOODING, a Quaker living in Devon, writes occasionally for *The Friend*. His doctoral thesis, 'Natural Strange Beatitudes', is dedicated to Graham Shaw, author of *God In Our Hands* (1987), and explores Geoffrey Hill's *The Orchards of Syon*.

HOWARD WRIGHT lectures in Design at Ulster University, Belfast. He was awarded second prize in 2018's Ver Poets Open and Commended in the McLellan Prize. Poems published in *The North* and *Cyphers*. Others are due to appear in *Stand* and *The Dalhousie Review*.

ARTIST

DAVID BROWN, after a career in mathematics and biology, studied printmaking, fine art and art history at Cambridge School of Art and at the London College of Communication. His passions as a printmaker are architecture – a passion ignited by a visit to Italy as a young student – and the abstract. He creates prints digitally, writing the scripts for each one in the JAVA processing language, citing Borromini, Hawksmoor, Seurat and Albers among those who inspire him in his own art and in the experimental methods he uses. He has work in private and public collections, including those of the Universities of London, Edinburgh and Cambridge, and of the V&A, and has exhibited widely in the UK and abroad.
Email: artist@davidbrownprintmaker.com

Printed in Great Britain
by Amazon